The only guides to compare the content and
st

Music, Drama & Dance

CRAC
Degree Course Guides
2007/08

CRAC
Career Development – FOR LIFE

The CRAC Series of Degree
Course Guides
Music, Drama and Dance

Compilers and series editors
Andrew Smith and Marion Owen

This Guide published in 2007 by
Trotman, an imprint of Crimson
Publishing, Westminster House,
Kew Road, Richmond, Surrey
TW9 2ND
www.crimsonpublishing.co.uk

Copyright © Trotman 2007

British Library Cataloguing in
Publication Data
A catalogue record for this book
is available from the British Library

ISBN 978-1-90604-115-1

Printed and bound in Great
Britain by Bell & Bain, Glasgow

This Degree Course Guide is one of a series providing comparative information about first-degree courses offered in the UK. The aim of the series is to help you choose the course most suitable for you.

This Guide is not an official publication, and although every effort has been made to ensure accuracy, the publishers can accept no responsibility for errors or omissions. Changes are continually being made and details have not been given for all courses, so you must also consult up-to-date prospectuses before finally deciding which courses to apply for. The publishers wish to thank the institutions of higher education that have provided information for this edition.

CRAC: The Careers Research and Advisory Centre

CRAC is an independent not-for-profit organisation. CRAC Degree Course Guides are published under exclusive licence by Trotman Publishing. For catalogues or information, write to Trotman Publishing; to buy publications, contact NBN International, Estover Road, Plymouth PL6 7PY. Tel: 0870 900 2665.

Academic consultants:

Music:
Professor Allan F Moore,
University of Surrey

Drama and Dance
Sara Reed, Dartington College of
Arts

Music, Drama and Dance

With the recent changes to student funding and tuition fees, entering higher education can no longer be a decision made lightly by school-leavers. Though overall there has been an increase in the numbers applying to university in the last five years, those numbers have fluctuated and the funding changes have muddied the waters for students who do not have the ready funds to enter, and leave, higher education debt-free.

So is it still worth it? There is evidence that there is still a 'graduate advantage'. Salaries for graduates across the span of a career remain higher than for non-graduates. The demand in the UK for higher skills is great; it is clear that higher levels of skills are associated with higher levels of productivity, and greater productivity coupled with higher-level skills are vital to the growth of the UK economy.

Career choices for graduates are constantly changing. Changes in industry mean that there is an increasing demand for graduates to enter marketing, IT, management accountancy, management consultancy, community and society occupations and other newer professions. Graduate career paths are not necessarily clear-cut, but the majority of graduates find themselves in employment that is related to their long-term career plans. One growing trend is that employers are more and more interested in work experience. The good news here is that universities are increasingly catering for this by providing assessed placements that form part of the degree course and opportunities for volunteering in the local community.

Students and graduates feel that their decision to enter higher education is worthwhile. The 2006 National Student Survey, the official survey of students' feelings about their courses, shows that approximately 80% were satisfied with their higher education compared to their expectations. According to the research project *Seven Years On: Graduate Careers in a Changing Labour Market*, more than two-thirds of graduates say they would do it all over again.

Thus it seems that the prospects for new entrants to higher education are still exciting. Making this decision may be daunting, bewildering or even liberating. It is vital that you take into account all of the factors that you feel are important in making a choice: your career aspirations, your abilities and aptitudes, the teaching facilities, opportunities for placements and, importantly, your passion for the subject. The choice of institutions and degree programmes is vast, and creating a shortlist can prove to be challenging – the biggest challenge being to ensure your choice of course and institution is an informed one. The CRAC *Degree Course Guides* are intended to be accurate, comprehensive and insightful to help equip you to do just this, making them essential reading for anyone considering entry to higher education.

Jeffrey Defries, Chief Executive
The Careers Research and Advisory Centre (CRAC)
www.crac.org.uk

The tables provide comparative information about first-degree courses offered at higher education institutions (universities and colleges) in the UK. Each table provides detailed information organised alphabetically by institution and course title. An at-a-glance summary of the material in each main table is given below:

Table 2a: First-degree courses
This gives the degree qualification, duration, foundation year availability, modes of study, whether the course is part of a modular scheme, course type and number of combined courses available.

Table 2b: Subjects in combination
This lists subjects that can be combined with music, drama or dance, and where they can be studied.

Tables 3a–3c: Course content
These give detailed information on the content and organisation of the courses, and special features such as practical experience.

Table 4: Assessment methods
This gives the frequency of assessment, years in which there are exams contributing to the final degree mark and percentage assessed by coursework.

Table 5: Entrance requirements
This gives the number of students on each course, typical offer in UCAS points, A-level grades and Scottish Highers, and required and preferred subjects at A-level.

'How to use this Guide' provides an overview of the book's content and more detailed information is provided before each table.

This Guide provides you with comparative information about the honours degree courses in music, drama and dance that you can take at higher education institutions in the UK. It aims to help you answer some of the questions you need to ask if you are going to find the courses that suit you best and interest you most. Some of these questions are shown below, with an indication of where you should look in the Guide for answers.

The first part of the Guide covers music, the second, drama and dance. The chapters are numbered from 1 in each part, so the following outline applies to all the parts.

What are these subjects like at degree level?   The first chapter is designed to give you some insight into what studying music, drama or dance is like at degree level. It gives an indication of what you will learn and how you will learn it, with an overview of the very wide variety of courses on offer. The chapter concludes with some advice about the careers you can enter with a degree in one of these subjects.

What courses are offered in music, drama and dance?   First you will need to decide whether a specialised or combined course will suit you best, and how long you want to spend on the course. You can get basic information on these points from TABLE 2a, which lists all courses in which one of these subjects can make up at least half of a degree course. TABLE 2b then shows which subjects you can combine with music, drama or dance in a two-subject degree.

At the end of Chapter 2 there is a list of courses in related areas, which may interest you as an alternative to a music, drama or dance course.

What are the courses like?   One of your major concerns will naturally be to find out just what you will study during your undergraduate career. Chapter 3 describes the style and content of the courses, mainly using tables so that you can compare courses easily. Before you dive into the tables, you should read the surrounding text, as this will tell you how to interpret them and what they can and cannot tell you.

How will my work be assessed?   Institutions in higher education use a wide variety of assessment methods, and the balance between them is often different at different institutions. Chapter 4 identifies and distinguishes between the approaches used.

What do I need to get accepted for a course?   Chapter 5 describes the qualifications you will need for admission to degree courses covered by this Guide, and TABLE 5 lists the requirements for individual courses and gives an indication of the number of places on offer. There is no simple relationship between the number of places on offer and how easy it is to get accepted for a course, but this figure does at least give you some idea of how many fellow students you would have on a course.

Where do I go from here?   This Guide, like the others in the series, aims to provide comparative information about courses to help you decide which ones you want to follow up in more detail, but it is only concerned with the content and organisation of the courses themselves. You will need to look at prospectuses, websites such as www.trotman.co.uk, and the institutions' own sites, shown in TABLE 2a, to find out about such things as tuition fees, accommodation, locality and student life at each institution. Chapter 6 gives a list of sources of further information, including a contact name for each course. In addition, most institutions welcome visits from potential students, and many run open days. Once you have applied, you may be invited for an interview, which will usually include an opportunity to look around the institution's facilities.

Part 1

Chapter 1: Introduction

For most of us, a world without music is hard to imagine. We are surrounded by it all day long: everything seems to bleep at us, announce its presence with a jingle, or attempt to hold our attention or manipulate our mood with music of some kind. All forms of entertainment seem to have an obligatory music element, from the background music played at sporting events to the full-blown score of a film. Electronic equipment is no longer content to hum quietly to itself in a corner, but feels the need to assert itself, be it the ring tone of a mobile phone or the zap, crackle and squelch of a computer game.

Somebody is responsible for all these sounds, whether the simplest of beeps or the most majestic of symphonies. We are all consumers of music, but some of us are also producers, able to organise otherwise random sounds to produce music. Schools attempt to give everyone the experience of making music, but only a few people ultimately prove to have the talent and application to make music their career. If you are such a person, and the potential and experience of sound and music-making continues to intrigue and excite you, a degree in music may be for you. You will need a high degree of technical proficiency, the willingness to collaborate with others and an aptitude for hard, disciplined work, right from the start.

Choosing a course Many of today's degree programmes are broadly based, covering music of all types and from many parts of the world, and including topics such as ethnomusicology and sound recording. To make the most of such courses, you will need an open mind and a readiness to experiment. At one time, the specialist colleges of music offered their own diplomas rather than degree courses. Now, however, courses at all kinds of institution lead to the award of a degree, although this does not mean that all courses have the same content or approach. Broadly speaking, all courses offer a mix of practical music-making and theoretical study, but you should investigate the balance between these on the courses you are interested in. The tables in Chapter 3 of this Guide will help you to do this. You should use prospectuses and course brochures to find out about the specialisms, areas of expertise and professional credits of the staff teaching the course: one-to-one contact is often important on a music course. You may be attracted by the presence on the staff of, say, a world authority on Beethoven, and while this may be invaluable for your orchestral studies, you may find the same person has to spend time teaching outside their specialism.

A career in music Even at this early stage, you should think carefully about why you want to study music at degree level, and what your plans are beyond study, when you enter the world of work. Very few musicians support themselves entirely from playing professionally, and even if you are lucky enough and talented enough to have the opportunity to do this, you need to ask yourself if you are temperamentally suited to such a career and way of life: most students enrol on their

3

degree thinking of themselves just as performers or composers, but graduate as rounded musicians. In any case, most professional musicians take on additional work such as teaching and session work, the latter often including types of music well away from their own preferences. However, there are skills and aptitudes associated with the study of music that readily transfer to other careers, not to mention the huge range of options available if you combine the study of music with another subject. Even a relatively specialised degree in 'music' can now embrace other related arts such as music theatre, as well as aspects of sociology, popular culture, women's studies, ethnic studies and so on, all proof of the growing awareness of the part music plays in our lives. New career opportunities open up almost daily for those with the right training, background and ideas.

What do music graduates do? Over 2,000 students graduate in music each year. Typically, more than a third of them go on to further training (well above the average for most subjects), either teacher training, professional music training, conversion training (into areas like computing or law) or (usually a smaller proportion) study for higher degrees. You should investigate further study options early in your final year, as there is competition for places and funding, and many students have to pay for their postgraduate studies themselves.

Teaching careers To teach in a state school you need first to become a qualified teacher, which graduates normally achieve by taking a one-year Postgraduate Certificate in Education (PGCE). Many music graduates choose to teach at secondary level, though another subject is often required in addition to music; others prefer to teach at primary level, where most will teach across the curriculum, though some may specialise in music.

Some music graduates decide to concentrate on instrumental or singing teaching and take a teaching or performance diploma. Armed with this they can become peripatetic teachers, travelling from school to school, though opportunities to do this depend very much on the contacts you make and on the policies of local education authorities. Many teach privately from home, though this can restrict your social life, since the usual times for lessons are evenings and weekends.

Teaching can be an attractive option for several reasons. Apart from enabling you to maintain and develop your interest in music, it may also give you the opportunity to conduct choirs, orchestras and ensembles, organise extracurricular activities such as trips to the opera or choir tours, and even practise your own skills in composition, orchestration and performance. Part-time teaching can also be a useful source of income if you are trying to make your way as a performer, or even when you have become established. For more information on teacher training, visit the Teacher Training Agency website at www.teach.gov.uk.

The musical performer, conductor or composer Earning a living as a professional performer requires an exceptional technical standard, plus tenacity and stamina, not to mention an element of luck. Fewer than one in ten music graduates will make a good living from performing. There are a few full-time posts for organists, mainly in the larger churches and cathedrals. Organists wishing to use their talents in a part-time capacity should have little difficulty in finding an opening in local churches, both playing for services and conducting choirs. Singers may also find work in cathedral choirs, though this is usually part-time only, and mostly for male voices. Professional choirs and choruses occasionally advertise vacancies, but may also take on extras for large-scale works. In the industry generally, vacancies are rarely advertised. Making contacts, networking, establishing a reputation and using your initiative are central to finding work. Particularly if you are an instrumentalist, don't turn up your nose at opportunities to work even with amateur groups of musicians in the early stages of your career. The Incorporated Society of Musicians produces useful information for those interested in performance careers: their website is at www.ism.org.

The career path to becoming a full-time conductor or composer is among the most difficult to follow. In the field of concert music, postgraduate study, and possibly success in a major competition, will be necessary in order to get yourself known. However, opportunities for composers in multimedia fields are increasing. Although a postgraduate qualification will again be useful, networking (and proving your competence working on, for example, short student-produced films) will be crucial.

Broadcasting   Working in broadcasting appeals to many music students. Studio managers, producers and production assistants, programme researchers, librarians and secretaries are needed. Recruitment into these jobs has always been highly competitive, and as the shape of the broadcasting industry changes, more of this work is being done by outside contractors or freelances rather than by employees of large organisations such as the BBC. Those interested in broadcasting need to gain as much experience as possible while on their degree by, for example, working for hospital radio, student television or helping out voluntarily at a local radio station.

Publishing, media and information work   Opportunities in music publishing and journalism are also very competitive and few in number. In the former, a postgraduate specialism together with an interest in the business side of publishing could help. Aspiring journalists will need experience and evidence of their writing skills, perhaps gained through writing for a student or local newspaper. Postgraduate journalism courses are worth considering, although there is stiff competition for places.

Each year a few musicians train as librarians or information scientists. A year's work experience is required, followed by a postgraduate training course. Once you are qualified, you can apply for jobs in academic libraries, municipal music libraries or the private sector.

Other opportunities   There are a number of other career opportunities related to music. Administration attracts quite a number of those going straight into employment. This includes arts or music administration, where you might start your career working in a box office, for one of the arts councils, for a concert agent or an Arts Centre. Experience such as organising concerts at college or of voluntary work in an

Arts Centre is vital when applying for a first job in arts administration. For more information on the world of arts administration, see the Arts Marketing Association's website: www.a-m-a.co.uk. Arts administration positions are difficult to come by, however, and a greater number of music graduates take other administrative jobs in local or central government, education or the health service.

Music therapy is an option if you would like to combine music with a caring career. Competence on an instrument is necessary, as is experience, usually gained on a voluntary basis, of working with relevant client groups, such as the disabled or those with learning difficulties. A postgraduate training course is then required. For further information, see the website of the British Society for Music Therapy: www.bsmt.org.

Other fields of work entered by music graduates include music retailing, acting as a publisher's representative visiting shops and schools, copying music ready for publishing (often on a freelance basis), and working for instrument makers and repairers.

Music

TABLE 2a lists the courses at universities and colleges in the UK that lead to the award of an honours degree in which you spend at least half of your time studying music. When the table was compiled it was as up to date as possible, but sometimes new courses are announced and existing courses withdrawn, so before you finally submit your application you should check the UCAS website, www.ucas.com, to make sure the courses you plan to apply for are still on offer.

Duration   The *Duration* column shows the duration of the course, including any time spent abroad or in employment (during a sandwich course), so courses with optional periods of this type will generally show two possible durations, for example '3, 4'. This indicates that a course can, for example:

- take three years' continuous study in the UK, or four years if the option for study abroad is taken
- be taken as a sandwich course or a straightforward full-time degree
- lead to alternative final degrees.

Sometimes several variants of a course are available, differing in length as well as in other features, so you should check with the institution to make sure you know exactly what is on offer.

Foundation years and franchised courses   The *Foundation year* column shows whether an optional foundation year is available if your qualifications are not in the relevant subjects for direct entry to the course. A foundation year allows you to acquire the necessary knowledge and skills to begin the main course on a par with students entering the course directly. Foundation years have been introduced mainly to encourage more students to follow science, engineering and mathematics, so are available mostly for those subjects.

Foundation years are not the same as Foundation Degrees. These are qualifications in their own right and are currently only offered in England, Wales and Northern Ireland. Courses leading to a Foundation Degree last two years and are particularly related to workplace skills. However, they can provide another route into honours degree courses, especially at the institutions offering them. For more information, see www.foundationdegree.org.uk.

Franchised courses   TABLE 2a also shows whether the foundation year can or must be taken at a franchised institution, which will typically be a college of further education in the same region. Some institutions also franchise complete degree courses, sometimes at colleges outside their immediate locality. Refer to prospectuses for further details of franchising arrangements.

Optional foundation years are not included in the *Duration* column, so you should add one to those figures to give the length including a foundation year.

Music

Direct entry to year 2 in Scotland   In Scotland, most students enter university with a broader and less specialised background than in the rest of the UK, so the first year is often similar in function to a foundation course. If you are well qualified, you may be able to gain exemption from this first year for some courses, particularly at the older Scottish universities. The *Foundation year* column shows courses for which this is possible, and in these cases the *Duration* figures should be reduced by one for direct entry to the second year.

Modes of study   The *Modes of study* column shows whether a course is available in full-time, part-time, sandwich or time abroad modes. The Guide does not include courses that are only available part time, but does show if courses are available part time in addition to one of the other modes.

Courses may be shown as involving time abroad for a number of reasons. The most straightforward is if the named course has an optional or compulsory period of study or work experience overseas. The period spent abroad will usually be about a year; courses in which you spend less than six months abroad do not qualify for the time abroad description. However, to avoid duplication of information, a time abroad entry may also mean that there is a variant of the course with a slightly different title (usually including a phrase such as 'with study in Europe' or 'International') and involving study or a work placement abroad. Note that a course is shown as including time abroad only when that opportunity arises *as part of the music course*. If time can be spent abroad only if you combine the study of music with a modern language, the course is not shown as a time abroad course in TABLE 2a.

Modular schemes   Many institutions offer modular schemes in which music can be studied alongside a wide range of other, often quite unrelated, subjects. Note that although many courses are described as 'modular', this usually means that the music content itself is organised in modules; a modular *course*, in this sense, may or may not be part of a modular *scheme*.

Modular schemes can give you much greater flexibility in choosing what you study and when, and have the particular benefit of allowing you to delay specialisation until you know more about the subject. However, there is a great deal of variation in the way modular schemes are organised, and there is always some restriction on the combination of modules you can take. If you feel strongly that you want to take a particular combination of subjects in a modular scheme, you should check prospectuses carefully, as some institutions do not guarantee that all advertised combinations will be available.

Course type   This Guide describes courses in which you can spend at least half of your time studying music. Specialised courses, in which you can spend substantially more than half of your time studying one of these subjects, are shown as ● in TABLE 2a. The *No of combined courses* column in TABLE 2a shows how many subjects are available to combine with music in a combined course. In these you spend between half and two-thirds of your time studying music, and the rest studying another subject. You can use TABLE 2b to find out where you can study a specific subject in combination with music (you should use the UCAS website or prospectuses if you want to know what combinations are available at a specific institution).

Some entries in TABLE 2a show that you can study music as a single-subject specialised course or in combination with other subjects. In general, information in later tables for these entries will be given for the specialised course, though in many cases it will apply equally to the combined courses.

Table 2a First-degree courses in **Music**

Institution / Course title	①②③ see combined subject list – Table 2b	Degree	Duration (Number of years)	Foundation year (● at this institution, ○ at franchised institution, ◑ second-year entry)	Modes of study (● full time; ▼ part time, ○ time abroad, ◑ sandwich)	Modular scheme	Course type (● specialised; ◑ combined)	No of combined courses
Aberdeen www.abdn.ac.uk								
Music		BMus	4		●		●	0
Music in Scotland		BMus	4		●		●	0
Anglia Ruskin www.anglia.ac.uk								
Audio and music technology		BSc	3		●		●	0
Creative music sound technology ①		BA	3		●		●◑	2
Music ②		BA	3	●	● ▼ ○	✿	●◑	4
Bangor www.bangor.ac.uk								
Music		BA/BMus	3		● ▼	✿	●◑	6
Bath Spa www.bathspa.ac.uk								
Creative music technology		BA	3		●		●	0
Music ①		BA	3		● ▼	✿	●◑	19
Bedfordshire www.beds.ac.uk								
Music technology		BA	3		●		●	0
Belfast www.qub.ac.uk								
Ethnomusicology ①		BA	3		●	✿	●◑	5
Music		BMus	3, 4		● ▼		●	0
Birmingham www.bham.ac.uk								
Music		BA/BMus	3		●		●◑	11
Brighton www.brighton.ac.uk								
Digital music		BA	3		●		●	0
Music and visual art ①		BA	3		● ▼	✿	◑	1
Bristol www.bris.ac.uk								
Music		BA	3		● ▼	✿	●	3
Bristol UWE www.uwe.ac.uk								
Creative music technology		BSc	3		●		●	0
Music technology ①		BSc	3		●		◑	12
Brunel www.brunel.ac.uk								
Creative music technology		BA	3, 4		● ◑		●	0
Music ①		BA	3		● ▼	✿	●◑	3
Cambridge www.cam.ac.uk								
Music		BA	3		●		●◑	1
Canterbury CC www.canterbury.ac.uk								
Commercial music		BA	3		●		●	0
Music ①		BA	3		● ▼	✿	●◑	31
Cardiff www.cardiff.ac.uk								
Music ①		BA	3, 4		● ○	✿	●◑	13
Music (BMus)		BMus	3		● ○		●	0
Central Lancashire www.uclan.ac.uk								
Music practice		BA	3		● ▼		●	0

(continued) Table 2a — First-degree courses in **Music**

Column groups: **Foundation year** — ● at this institution, ○ at franchised institution, ◑ second-year entry. **Modes of study** — ● full time; ▬ part time, ○ time abroad, ● sandwich. ✷ **Modular scheme**. **Course type** — ● specialised; ◐ combined. No of combined courses. (① ② ③ see combined subject list – Table 2b)

Institution / Course title	Degree	Duration (years)	Foundation: at this inst.	Foundation: at franchised inst.	Foundation: 2nd-year entry	Modes: full/part time	Time abroad	Sandwich	Modular scheme	Course type	No. of combined courses
Chester www.chester.ac.uk											
Media (commercial music production) ①	BA	3				●			✷	● ◐	10
Popular music ②	BA	3				● ▬			✷	● ◐	23
Chichester www.chiuni.ac.uk											
Music ①	BA	3				● ▬			✷	● ◐	14
Music with instrumental/vocal teaching	BA	3				● ▬				●	0
City www.city.ac.uk											
Music	BMus/BSc	3				●				● ◐	1
Colchester I www.colch-inst.ac.uk											
Music	BA	3	●			● ▬	○			●	0
Coventry www.coventry.ac.uk											
E-music	BSc	3				●				●	0
Music and professional practice	BA	3				●				●	0
Music composition and professional practice	BA	3				● ▬				●	0
Music technology	BSc	3, 4	●			●				●	0
Dartington CA www.dartington.ac.uk											
Music	BA	3				●			✷	● ◐	6
De Montfort www.dmu.ac.uk											
Music technology and innovation	BA	3				● ▬				●	0
Derby www.derby.ac.uk											
Popular music (production)	BA/BSc	3				● ▬			✷	◐	12
Doncaster C www.don.ac.uk											
Creative music technology	BA	3				●				●	0
Durham www.durham.ac.uk											
Music	BA	3				●				●	0
East Anglia www.uea.ac.uk											
Music	BA	3				● ▬			✷	● ◐	2
East London www.uel.ac.uk											
Music culture: theory and production	BA	3	●	○		● ▬				● ◐	5
Edinburgh www.ed.ac.uk											
History of art and history of music ①	MA	4				●				◐	1
Music ②	BMus	4			◑	● ▬				● ◐	1
Music technology	BMus	4				●				●	0
Glamorgan www.glam.ac.uk											
Music technology	BSc	3, 4				●		●		●	0
Popular music ①	BA	3				●				● ◐	2
Glasgow www.gla.ac.uk											
Music (BMus)	BMus	4			◑	● ▬	○			●	0
Music (MA) ①	MA	4, 5			◑	● ▬	○		✷	● ◐	38
Gloucestershire www.glos.ac.uk											
Popular music	BA	3				●				●	0
Goldsmiths www.goldsmiths.ac.uk											
Music	BMus	3	●			●				●	0
Popular music studies	BMus	3				●				●	0
Grimsby IFHE www.grimsby.ac.uk											
Creative music and digital media studies	BA	3				●				◐	1
Guildhall S Music & Drama www.gsmd.ac.uk											
Music	BMus	4				●				●	0

Institution / Course title	Degree	Duration (No. of years)	Foundation year	At this institution	At franchised institution	Second-year entry	Full time ● / part time ►	Time abroad	Sandwich	Modular scheme	Course type (specialised ● / combined ◐)	No of combined courses
Hertfordshire www.herts.ac.uk												
Electronic music ①	BSc	3		●			● ►			✇	● ◐	16
Music composition and technology	BSc	3		●			●				●	0
Music technology	BSc	3		●			●				●	0
Music, commercial composition and technology	BSc	3		●			●				●	0
Huddersfield www.hud.ac.uk												
Creative music technology	BMus	3		●			●				●	0
Music ①	BMus	3		●			●				● ◐	5
Music technology ②	BA	3		●			●				● ◐	2
Popular music	BA	3		●			●				●	0
Popular music production	BA	3, 4		●			●		◐		●	0
Hull www.hull.ac.uk												
Creative music technology ①	BA	3		●			● ►			✇	● ◐	2
Jazz and popular music	BA	3		●			●				●	0
Music ②	BMus/BA	3		●			●				● ◐	7
Music technology and computing ③	BSc	3		●			●				◐	1
Keele www.keele.ac.uk												
Music ①	BA/BSc	3	●				●			✇	◐	29
Music technology ②	BA/BSc	3	●				●			✇	◐	29
Kent www.ukc.ac.uk												
Music technology	BSc	3		●			●				●	0
King's College London www.kcl.ac.uk												
Music	BMus/BA	3		●			●				● ◐	2
Kingston www.kingston.ac.uk												
Creative music technologies	BMus	3		●			●				●	0
Music ①	BMus	3		●			●				● ◐	6
Music composition	BMus	3		●			●				●	0
Music performance	BMus	3		●			●				●	0
Popular musics	BMus	3		●			●				●	0
Lancaster www.lancs.ac.uk												
Music ①	BA/BMus	3		●			●				● ◐	7
Music technology	BA	3		●			●				●	0
Musicology	BA	3		●			●				●	0
Leeds www.leeds.ac.uk												
Music ①	BA/BMus	3, 4		●			● ►	O		✇	● ◐	12
Popular and world musics	BA	3, 4		●			●	O			●	0
Leeds C Music www.lcm.ac.uk												
Jazz studies	BA	3	●				●				●	0
Music	BA	3	●				●				●	0
Music production	BA	3		●			●				●	0
Popular music studies	BA	3		●			●				●	0
Leeds Metropolitan www.lmu.ac.uk												
Creative music and sound technology	BSc	3, 4		●			● ►	◐			●	0
Liverpool www.liv.ac.uk												
Music ①	BA	3		●			●			✇	● ◐	1
Popular music ②	BA	3		●			●				● ◐	2
Liverpool Hope www.hope.ac.uk												
Music ①	BA	3		●			● ►			✇	● ◐	27
Music, popular music, music technology	BA	3		●			●				●	0

First-degree courses in **Music**

Institution / Course title	①②③ see combined subject list – Table 2b	Degree	Duration (Number of years)	Foundation year	Modes of study	Modular scheme	Course type	No of combined courses
LIPA www.lipa.ac.uk								
Music		BA	3		●		●	0
Performing arts (music)		BA	3		● ➥		●	0
Sound technology		BA	3		●		●	0
Liverpool John Moores www.ljmu.ac.uk								
Popular music studies		BA	3		●		●	0
London Metropolitan www.londonmet.ac.uk								
Musical instruments		BA	3		●		● ◐	8
Manchester www.man.ac.uk								
Music		MusB	3		●		● ◐	1
Manchester Metropolitan www.mmu.ac.uk								
Music ①		BA	3		● ➥	☻	◐	24
Music studies ②		BA	3		●	☻	◐	21
Popular musics ③		BA	3		●	☻	◐	23
Sonic arts ④		BA	3		●	☻	◐	23
Middlesex www.mdx.ac.uk								
Jazz		BA	3		● ➥		●	0
Music ①		BA	3		● ➥	☻	● ◐	12
Napier www.napier.ac.uk								
Music		BMus	4	◐	●		●	0
Popular music		BA	4		●		●	0
Newcastle www.ncl.ac.uk								
Folk and traditional music		BMus	4	●	● ➥ ○	☻	●	0
Music		BA/BMus	3, 4		● ➥ ○	☻	●	0
Newcastle C www.ncl-coll.ac.uk								
Popular, jazz and commercial music		BMus	3		●		●	0
Northampton www.northampton.ac.uk								
Creative digital music		BA	3		●		● ◐	27
Northbrook C www.northbrook.ac.uk								
Music composition for professional media		BA	3		●		●	0
Music production: music technology		BA	3		●		●	0
Music technology		BSc	3		●		●	0
Popular music		BA	3		●		●	0
Nottingham www.nottingham.ac.uk								
Music		BA	3		● ➥		● ◐	2
Oxford www.ox.ac.uk								
Music		BA	3		●		●	0
Oxford Brookes www.brookes.ac.uk								
Music		BA/BSc	3, 4		● ➥	☻	● ◐	47
Paisley www.paisley.ac.uk								
Commercial music		BA	4		●		●	0
Music technology		BSc	4		●		●	0
Plymouth www.plymouth.ac.uk								
Music ①		BA	3		●		● ◐	1
Sonic arts		BA	3		●		●	0
Portsmouth www.port.ac.uk								
Music and sound technology		BSc	3, 4		● ◐		●	0
Roehampton www.roehampton.ac.uk								
Music		BMus/BA/BSc	3	●	● ➥ ○	☻	● ◐	22

First-degree courses in Music

Institution / Course title	① ② ③ see combined subject list – Table 2b	Degree	Duration Number of years	Foundation year ● at this institution ○ at franchised institution ◑ second-year entry	Modes of study ● full time; ➤ part time ○ time abroad ◑ sandwich	Modular scheme 🕐	Course type ● specialised; ◑ combined	No of combined courses
Rose Bruford C www.bruford.ac.uk								
Actor-musician ①		BA	3		●		◑	1
Music technology		BA	3		●		●	0
Royal Academy of Music www.ram.ac.uk								
Music		BMus	4		● ○		●	0
Royal C Music www.rcm.ac.uk								
Music		BMus	4	●	●		●	0
Royal Holloway www.rhul.ac.uk								
Music		BMus/BA	3	●	●	🕐	● ◑	10
Royal N C Music www.rncm.ac.uk								
Performance/composition		BMus/GradRNCM	4		●		●	0
Royal Scottish A Music & Drama www.rsamd.ac.uk								
Music		BMus	4	◑	●		●	0
Scottish music		BA	4		●		●	0
Scottish music (piping)		BA	4		●		●	0
Royal Welsh C Music & Drama www.rwcmd.ac.uk								
Music		BMus	4		●		●	0
Salford www.salford.ac.uk								
Music		BA	3		●		●	0
Popular music and recording		BA	3		●		●	0
Sheffield www.sheffield.ac.uk								
Music ①		BMus/BA	3, 4		● ○		● ◑	10
Traditional music with folklore studies		BA	3		●		●	0
SOAS www.soas.ac.uk								
Music studies		BA	3		●	🕐	● ◑	26
Southampton www.soton.ac.uk								
Music		BA/BSc	3		● ➤		● ◑	6
Southampton Solent www.solent.ac.uk								
Digital music		BA	3		●		●	0
Popular music and record production		BA	3		●		●	0
Popular music performance		BA	3		●		●	0
Urban and electronic music		BA	3		●		●	0
Staffordshire www.staffs.ac.uk								
Music technology		BSc	3, 4		● ◑		● ◑	1
Strathclyde www.strath.ac.uk								
Applied music		BA	4	◑	●	🕐	●	0
Sunderland www.sunderland.ac.uk								
Music		BA	3		●		◑	23
Surrey www.surrey.ac.uk								
Music		BMus	3, 4		● ○ ◑		●	0
Music and sound recording (Tonmeister)		BMus	4		● ◑		●	0
Music with computer sound design		BMus	3		●		●	0
Sussex www.sussex.ac.uk								
Music		BA	3		●		● ◑	7
Swansea IHE www.sihe.ac.uk								
Music technology		BSc	3		●		●	0
Teesside www.tees.ac.uk								
Digital music creation		BA	3, 4		● ◑		●	0

Music

(continued) Table 2a — First-degree courses in **Music** Institution / Course title	see combined subject list – Table 2b	Degree	Duration Number of years	Foundation year ● at this institution ○ at franchised institution ◐ second-year entry	Modes of study ● full time; ➤ part time ○ time abroad ◐ sandwich	Modular scheme	Course type ● specialised; ◐ combined	No of combined courses
Thames Valley www.tvu.ac.uk								
Music ①		BA	3	●	●		◐	3
Music (performance/composition)		BMus	3		●		●	0
Music technology		BA	3		●		●	0
Popular music performance		BMus	3		●		●	0
Trinity C Music www.tcm.ac.uk								
Music		BMus	4		●		●	0
Truro C www.trurocollege.ac.uk								
Contemporary world jazz		BA	3		●		●	0
UCE Birmingham www.uce.ac.uk								
Music technology		BSc	3, 4		● ◐		●	0
UCE Birmingham Conservatoire www.conservatoire.uce.ac.uk								
Jazz		BMus	4		●		●	0
Music		BMus	4		●		●	0
Ulster www.ulster.ac.uk								
Music		BMus	3	●	●		● ◐	7
Wales (UWIC) www.uwic.ac.uk								
Music and audioelectronic systems		BSc	3		● ➤		◐	1
Westminster www.wmin.ac.uk								
Commercial music		BA	3		●		●	0
Commercial music performance		BA	3		●		●	0
Wolverhampton www.wlv.ac.uk								
Music ①		BA	3		● ➤	✿	● ◐	6
Popular music ②		BA	3		● ➤	✿	● ◐	6
York www.york.ac.uk								
Music		BA	3		●		●	0
York St John www.yorksj.ac.uk								
Music ①		BA	3		●		◐	7
Performance: music		BA	3		● ➤		●	0

Subjects available in combination with music TABLE 2b shows subjects that can make up between a third and half of your programme of study in combination with music in the combined degrees listed in TABLE 2a. For example, if you are interested in combining music with geography, first look up geography in the list to find the institutions offering geography in combination with music. You can then use the index number given after the institution name to find which of the courses at the institution can be combined with geography. If there is no index number after an institution's name in TABLE 2b, that is because there is only one course at that institution in the appropriate part of TABLE 2a.

It is not possible to describe in the space available here the many different ways in which combined courses are organised, so you should read prospectuses carefully. For example, you should find out if the subjects are taught independently of each other or if they are integrated in any way. Combined courses in modular schemes often provide considerable flexibility, allowing you to vary the proportions of the subjects and include elements of other subjects. However, this means that you may lose some of the benefits of more integrated courses.

Note that the names given in the table for the combined subjects have been standardised to make comparison and selection easier. This means that the name used at a particular institution may not be exactly the same as that given in the table. However, in nearly all cases it will be very similar, so you should not find much difficulty in identifying a particular course combination when you look at the prospectus.

Table 2b

Music

Subjects to combine with **Music**

Accountancy/accounting Northampton, Oxford Brookes
Acoustics Southampton
Advertising Chester①
African/Caribbean studies SOAS
American studies Canterbury CC①, Derby, Keele① ②, Manchester Metropolitan① ② ③ ④, Sunderland
Anthropology Glasgow①, Oxford Brookes, Roehampton
Applied social science Manchester Metropolitan① ② ③ ④
Arabic SOAS
Archaeology Glasgow①
Art Bath Spa①, Canterbury CC①
Art history Edinburgh①, Glasgow①, Kingston①, Leeds①, Northampton, Oxford Brookes, Roehampton, SOAS
Artificial intelligence Bristol UWE①, Leeds①, Oxford Brookes
Arts management Dartington CA, Manchester Metropolitan①, Middlesex①, Oxford Brookes
Astronomy Hertfordshire①
Astrophysics Keele① ②
Audiotechnology Bristol UWE①, Huddersfield②, Wales (UWIC)
Biblical studies Sheffield①
Biochemistry Keele①
Biological sciences Canterbury CC①
Biology Bath Spa①, Derby, Keele②, Oxford Brookes, Roehampton
Burmese SOAS
Business computing Canterbury CC①, Keele① ②
Business information systems East London
Business studies Bath Spa①, Bristol UWE①, Canterbury CC①, Chester① ②, Chichester①, Derby, Glasgow①, Hertfordshire①, Hull①, Keele②, Liverpool Hope①, London Metropolitan, Manchester Metropolitan① ② ③ ④, Northampton, Oxford Brookes, Sunderland, Wolverhampton②
Celtic Glasgow①
Chemistry Keele① ②, Sunderland

Childhood studies Canterbury CC①, Liverpool Hope①, Manchester Metropolitan① ② ③ ④, Oxford Brookes, Roehampton
Chinese SOAS
Chinese studies Sheffield①
Classical studies Birmingham, Glasgow①, Roehampton
Communication studies Anglia Ruskin③, Bath Spa①, Canterbury CC①, Chester②, London Metropolitan, Oxford Brookes, York St John①
Comparative literature Glasgow①
Computer science Chester① ②, City, Keele① ②, Lancaster①
Computing Canterbury CC①, East Anglia, Glasgow①, Hertfordshire①, Hull①, King's College London, Leeds①, Liverpool Hope①, Northampton, Oxford Brookes, Sunderland
Creative writing Bath Spa①, Chichester①, Manchester Metropolitan① ② ③ ④, Roehampton, Wolverhampton②
Criminology Canterbury CC①, Keele①, Manchester Metropolitan① ② ③ ④, Northampton, Roehampton, Sunderland
Cultural studies Bath Spa①, Cardiff①, Derby, East London, Manchester Metropolitan① ② ③ ④, Sussex
Czech Glasgow①
Dance Bath Spa①, Chester②, Chichester①, Dartington CA, Derby, Hull①, Liverpool Hope①, Manchester Metropolitan① ② ③ ④, Northampton, Roehampton, Sunderland, Ulster, Wolverhampton②
Design York St John①
Development studies Chester②, SOAS
Drama Anglia Ruskin③, Bath Spa①, Birmingham, Bristol UWE①, Brunel①, Chester②, Huddersfield①, Hull②, Kingston①, Liverpool Hope①, Manchester, Manchester Metropolitan① ② ③ ④, Middlesex①, Northampton, Roehampton, Rose Bruford C①, Royal Holloway, Ulster, Wolverhampton① ②
East Asian studies Sheffield①
East European studies Glasgow①
Ecology Oxford Brookes
Economic/social history Glasgow①

15

Subjects to combine with **Music**

Economics   Bristol UWE①, Glasgow①, Hertfordshire①, Keele① ②, London Metropolitan, Oxford Brookes

Education   Cambridge, Chester②, Derby, Keele①②, Liverpool Hope①, Manchester Metropolitan① ② ③ ④, Middlesex①, Northampton, Oxford Brookes, Plymouth①, Roehampton, Sunderland, Wolverhampton①, York St John①

English   Anglia Ruskin②, Belfast①, Birmingham, Brunel①, Canterbury CC①, Chester②, Chichester①, Huddersfield①, Hull①, Keele①, Leeds①, Manchester Metropolitan① ② ③ ④, Northampton, Oxford Brookes, Sheffield①, Southampton, Sunderland, Wolverhampton① ②

English as a foreign language Chichester①

English language   Canterbury CC①, Glasgow①, Hertfordshire ①, Oxford Brookes, Roehampton

English literature   Bath Spa①, Cardiff①, Glasgow①, Lancaster①, Liverpool Hope①, Middlesex①, Roehampton, York St John①

Enterprise/entrepreneurship Chichester①, London Metropolitan, Northampton

Environmental management   Liverpool Hope①

Environmental science   Canterbury CC①, Oxford Brookes

Environmental studies   Hertfordshire①

European studies   Bristol UWE①, Sunderland

Exercise science   Oxford Brookes

Film/television studies   Anglia Ruskin①, Bath Spa①, Brunel①, Canterbury CC①, Chester①, Derby, East London, Glamorgan①, Glasgow①, Hull①, Kingston①, Liverpool Hope①, Manchester Metropolitan① ② ③, Middlesex①, Oxford Brookes, Roehampton, Sussex, York St John①

Finance   East London, Keele① ②

Fine art   Chester②, Liverpool Hope①, Northampton, York St John①

Food studies   Bath Spa①

Forensic science   Canterbury CC①, Keele① ②

French   Bangor, Bristol, Canterbury CC①, Cardiff①, Chester②, Glasgow①, Hertfordshire①, Hull①, Keele① ②, Leeds①, Middlesex①, Northampton, Roehampton, Royal Holloway, Sheffield①, Southampton, Sussex, Ulster

French studies   Birmingham, Lancaster①, Oxford Brookes

Gender studies   Sunderland

Geographical information systems Bath Spa①

Geography   Bath Spa①, Canterbury CC①, Glasgow①, Keele① ②, Manchester

Metropolitan① ② ③ ④, Oxford Brookes, SOAS, Sunderland

Geology   Keele①

Georgian   SOAS

German   Bangor, Bristol, Cardiff①, Chester②, Glasgow①, Hull①, King's College London, Leeds①, Middlesex①, Nottingham, Royal Holloway, Sheffield①, Southampton, Sussex, Ulster

German studies   Birmingham, Lancaster①

Graphic design   Chester① ②

Greek   Glasgow①

Hausa   SOAS

Health studies   Bath Spa①, Liverpool Hope①, Manchester Metropolitan① ② ③ ④, Northampton, Sunderland

Hebrew   SOAS

Hindi   SOAS

Hispanic studies   Birmingham, Glasgow①, Sheffield①

History   Bath Spa①, Birmingham, Canterbury CC①, Cardiff①, Chester②, Chichester①, Derby, Glamorgan②, Glasgow①, Huddersfield①, Keele①, Lancaster①, Leeds①, Liverpool Hope①, Northampton, Oxford Brookes, Royal Holloway, SOAS, Sunderland

Hospitality management   Oxford Brookes

Human biology   Hertfordshire①, Liverpool Hope①, Oxford Brookes, Roehampton

Human geography   Hertfordshire①, Keele① ②, Northampton

Human resource management   Keele①, Manchester Metropolitan① ② ③ ④, Northampton

Indonesian   SOAS

Information systems   Keele① ②, Oxford Brookes

Information technology   Kingston①, Liverpool Hope①, Manchester Metropolitan① ② ③ ④, Middlesex①

International studies/relations Keele① ②, Oxford Brookes

Internet technology   Bristol UWE①, Canterbury CC①, Kingston①

Irish   Ulster

Irish studies   Liverpool Hope①

Italian   Bangor, Bristol, Cardiff①, Glasgow①, Hull①, Leeds①, Middlesex①, Royal Holloway, Sussex

Italian studies   Birmingham, Lancaster①

Japanese   SOAS

Japanese studies   Oxford Brookes

Journalism   Canterbury CC①, Chester① ②, Huddersfield①, Roehampton, Sunderland

Korean   SOAS

Korean studies   Sheffield①

Latin   Glasgow①

Law   Keele① ②, Liverpool Hope①, Northampton, Oxford Brookes

Legal studies   Canterbury CC①, Manchester Metropolitan① ② ③ ④

Leisure management Oxford Brookes
Leisure studies Liverpool Hope①
Linguistics Belfast①, Bristol UWE①, SOAS, Sunderland
Management science Hertfordshire①, Keele②
Management studies Chester① ②, Northampton, Royal Holloway, Southampton, Staffordshire
Marketing Bristol UWE①, Canterbury CC①, Chester①, Derby, Keele②, Liverpool Hope①, London Metropolitan, Manchester Metropolitan① ② ③ ④, Northampton, Oxford Brookes
Mathematics Birmingham, Bristol UWE①, East Anglia, Edinburgh②, Glasgow①, Keele①, Kingston①, Leeds①, Northampton, Oxford Brookes, Royal Holloway, Southampton
Media studies Canterbury CC①, Chichester①, Grimsby IFHE, Keele① ②, Liverpool②, Middlesex①, Northampton, Sunderland, Thames Valley①
Medicinal chemistry Keele① ②
Medieval studies Canterbury CC①
Modern languages Huddersfield①
Molecular biology Oxford Brookes
Multimedia Bristol UWE①, Chester① ②, Hertfordshire①, London Metropolitan, Oxford Brookes, Thames Valley①
Music Anglia Ruskin①, Belfast①, Keele②, Liverpool②, Manchester Metropolitan③ ④, Wolverhampton②
Music technology Chichester①, Derby, Keele①, Wolverhampton②
Nepali SOAS
Neuroscience Keele②
Nutrition Liverpool Hope①, Oxford Brookes
Performance studies Chester②, Chichester①, Dartington CA, East London, Northampton, Oxford Brookes
Persian SOAS
Philosophy Cardiff①, Glasgow①, Hertfordshire①, Keele②, Leeds①, Liverpool Hope①, Manchester Metropolitan① ② ③ ④, Middlesex①, Northampton, Nottingham, Oxford Brookes, Roehampton, Sheffield①, Sussex
Photography Chester②, Roehampton
Physical geography Keele① ②, Oxford Brookes
Physics Cardiff①, Glasgow①, Hertfordshire①, Keele① ②
Physiology Sunderland
Polish Glasgow①
Politics Belfast①, Canterbury CC①, Cardiff①, Glasgow①, Keele①, Liverpool Hope①, Oxford Brookes, Royal Holloway, Sunderland

Psychology Anglia Ruskin②, Bath Spa①, Canterbury CC①, Chester②, Derby, Glasgow①, Keele① ②, Leeds①, Liverpool Hope①, Manchester Metropolitan① ② ③ ④, Oxford Brookes, Roehampton, Royal Holloway, Sunderland, Ulster
Public policy Glasgow①
Public relations Sunderland
Publishing Oxford Brookes
Pure mathematics Cardiff①
Religious studies Bangor, Bath Spa①, Canterbury CC①, Cardiff①, Oxford Brookes, Roehampton, SOAS
Retailing Oxford Brookes
Russian Glasgow①, Sheffield①
Russian studies Birmingham
Scottish history Glasgow①
Scottish literature Glasgow①
Social anthropology Belfast①, SOAS
Social philosophy Cardiff①
Sociology Bath Spa①, Canterbury CC①, Chester②, Derby, Glasgow①, Keele①, Liverpool Hope①, London Metropolitan, Manchester Metropolitan① ②, Northampton, Oxford Brookes, Sunderland
Software engineering Oxford Brookes
South Asian studies SOAS
South East Asian studies SOAS
Spanish Bangor, Chester②, Hertfordshire①, Hull②, Middlesex①, Roehampton, Royal Holloway, Sussex, Ulster
Spanish studies Lancaster①
Sports science Canterbury CC①
Sports studies Chester①, Hertfordshire①, Liverpool Hope①, Manchester Metropolitan① ② ③ ④, Northampton, Oxford Brookes
Statistics Hertfordshire①, Oxford Brookes
TEFL Sunderland
Textile design Bath Spa①
Thai SOAS
Theatre studies Dartington CA, Glasgow①
Theology Birmingham, Canterbury CC①, Chester②, Chichester①, Glasgow①, Leeds①, Liverpool Hope①, Oxford Brookes, Roehampton, York St John①
Third world studies Northampton
Tourism Canterbury CC①, Liverpool Hope①, Northampton, Oxford Brookes, Sunderland
Turkish SOAS
Urdu SOAS
Vietnamese SOAS
Visual art Brighton①, Dartington CA
War studies Liverpool Hope①
Welsh Bangor, Cardiff①

Music

Other courses that may interest you   Apart from the courses covered in other parts of this Guide, there are some courses that do not quite fit into any of the Guides in this series. The following courses are closely related to those in this part of the Guide, so if you are interested in music, you should perhaps consider these as well. They include courses where you spend less than half your time studying music, as well as courses providing a more intensive study of a specialised aspect of the subject.

- Music, multimedia and electronics (Leeds)
- Physics with studies in musical performance (Imperial College London)
- Music industry management (Buckinghamshire Chilterns UC)
- Music and media management (London Metropolitan)
- Music production (SE Essex C)
- Studio recording and performance technology (North East Wales I)
- Digital music (Teesside).

All the courses listed in TABLE 2a include, with varying emphasis, some form of practical work, composition, music history and analysis. The commonest pattern of courses is to have two general years followed by a final year in which you specialise in one of these areas, but there are different models. As music technology has developed dramatically, over the past few years, the time spent on these 'core' areas has sometimes diminished.

General vs specialised courses   As you read prospectuses and the tables in this and other chapters, you will come across a number of more specialised courses, such as Folk and traditional music, Jazz studies or Electronic music. Other courses may not declare a focus or emphasis in their titles, but it does not follow that they do not have a very clear identity and personality. No course could adequately cover all aspects of music, so there has to be some kind of selection to produce a coherent body of knowledge and skills to be studied. Look carefully at the balance of practical and theoretical work, how broad or narrow the historical perspective is, how much emphasis is laid on your creativity, the technical resources of the department and the areas of expertise of teaching staff. Then you will be able to make an informed choice of likely courses.

Practical work   An aspect of almost any music course is the continued development of your skills as a player or composer. Such work leads to performance and the examination of your musicality in performance. So score-reading, harmonisation, playing from figured bass, improvisation, transposition, orchestrating and arranging may all figure in examinations. In their final year many courses expect each student to present a recital or portfolio of their work. These should be seen as opportunities and challenges to be taken up with relish. They should grow naturally out of the range of ensemble playing, composition work and general music-making fostered in the first two years. Lively departments have tutorial staff who are themselves practising musicians and composers, and they will also regularly invite professional musicians to lecture, teach or perform.

Production   The rise in music technology which has come about since the invention of digital media has expanded the curriculum such that there are now whole degree programmes in music technology (some have titles such as sound recording or audio technology). Aspects of music technology also find their way onto more traditional degrees. These may be open to all students, but some programmes require facility with some mathematics, physics or electronics for study at greater depth. This area can cover everything from microphone placement (for live or studio recordings) to final mix-down and will usually address sequencing and sampling.

TABLE 3a gives information about the practical and production work covered in each of the courses.

Music

Table 3a

Course content: performance, composition and production

Key: O optional; ● compulsory; ◐ compulsory + options
①②③: see notes after table

Institution	Course title	Solo instrument	Solo singing	Choir	Improvisation	Orchestra	Small ensemble	Conducting	Imitative exercises	Original work	Orchestration	Electronic music	Popular music	Classical music	Electronic music	Multimedia	Live music	Studio production
		Performance							**Composition**				**Music production/recording**					
Anglia Ruskin	Audio and music technology									O	O	O	O	O	O	O	O	O
	Music ①	O	O	O		O	O	O	◐	◐		◐	O	O	O			
Bangor	Music ①	O	O			O	O		O	O	O	O	O	O	O			O
Bath Spa	Creative music technology									●		●				●	●	O
	Music ①	◐	O	●	O	●	●	◐	◐	◐	◐	◐						
Belfast	Ethnomusicology						●											
	Music	O	O	O		O	O	O	◐	O	O	O						
Birmingham	Music ①	O	O	O		O	O	O	◐	◐	O	◐						
Brighton	Digital music									●	◐	●	O		●	O	O	●
	Music and visual art		◐				◐			●		◐	◐				◐	◐
Bristol	Music	O	O			O	O	O	◐	◐	O	◐						
Brunel	Creative music technology									●	●	●	O	O	●	O	O	
	Music	O	O	◐		O	◐	O	◐	◐	◐	◐						
Cambridge	Music	O	O						●	O								
Canterbury CC	Music	O	O			O	O	O	O	O	O	O						
Cardiff	Both courses	O	O			O	O	O	●	O	O							
Central Lancashire	Music practice ①	O	O		●	O	O	●		●	O	O	O		O		●	●
Chester	Popular music	●			●		●						●				●	●
Chichester	Music	◐	◐	O	O	◐	●	O	◐	●	◐	O	O	O	O	O	●	O
	Music with instrumental/vocal teaching	O	O	O	O	O	O	O	O	O	O	O	O	O	O	O	●	O
City	Music ①	O	O	◐		◐	◐	O		●	O	●						
Colchester I	Music	●	O	O		O	O	O	O	O	O	O						
Coventry	Music and professional practice	●	O	●	●	O	●	O	●		●	O						
	Music composition and professional practice	O	O	●	●	O	●	O	●	●	●	O						
Dartington CA	Music	O	O	O		O	O	O	O	O	O	O						
De Montfort	Music technology and innovation				●					●		●			●	●	O	●
Derby	Popular music (production)	O	O	O		O	O		O	O	O	O	O		O		O	O
Durham	Music	O	O				O	O	●	O	O	O						
East Anglia	Music	O	O			O	O	O	O	O	O	O						
Edinburgh	History of art and history of music	O	O						O	O	O	O						
	Music	◐	O						O	O	●	O						
Glasgow	Music (BMus)	●	O			O	O	O	●	●	●	O			O	O		
	Music (MA) ①	O	O			O	O	O	O	O	O	O			O	O		
Goldsmiths	Music	◐	◐	◐		◐	◐		●	●	●	●						
	Popular music studies ①	●			●		●			●		O	●				●	●
Grimsby IFHE	Creative music and digital media studies	O	O	O	◐	O	◐	◐	◐	●	◐	◐	◐	◐	◐	◐	◐	◐
Guildhall S Music & Drama	Music	●	●			●	●	●		●	●	●						
Hertfordshire	Electronic music ①			●		●	●			●	●	●						
	Music composition and technology ②		O			◐	O			◐	O					●	◐	
	Music technology														◐	●	◐	
	Music, commercial composition and technology ③		O			◐	O			◐	O	◐				●	◐	●
Huddersfield	Music ①	◐	◐	◐	●	◐	◐	◐	O	◐	◐	◐						

Course content: performance, composition and production

Legend: ○ optional; ● compulsory; ◐ compulsory + options; ①②: see notes after table

Institution	Course title	Solo instrument	Solo singing	Choir	Improvisation	Orchestra	Small ensemble	Conducting	Imitative exercises	Original work	Orchestration	Electronic music	Popular music	Classical music	Electronic music	Multimedia	Live music	Studio production
Hull	Creative music technology ①	●		○		○	○		●	●	●	○						
	Music	○	○	◐	○	◐	○	◐		○	○	○	○	○	○	○	○	○
	Music technology and computing ②															●		●
Keele	Music	◐	○	○		○	○	○	◐	○	○	○						
	Music technology ①									○	●	●	○	○	●	○	○	
King's College London	Music ①	◐	◐	●		●	●	○	◐	○								
Kingston	Creative music technologies	○			○			○	○	●	○	●	○	○	●	○	○	●
	Music	○	○	○	○	○	○	○	○	○	○	○	○	○	○	○	○	○
	Music composition	○	○	○	○	○	○	○	○	●	●	○	○	○	○	○	○	○
	Music performance	○	○	○	○	○	○	○	○	○	○	○	○	○	○	○	○	○
	Popular musics	○	○	○	●	○	○	○	○	○	●	○	○	○	○	○	○	○
Leeds	Music	●	○	○		●	●	●	●	●	●	●						
	Popular and world musics ①	○	○	○		○	○	○	○	○	○	○						
Leeds C Music	Jazz studies	●	○	○		●	●	○	●	●	●	●						
	Music	●	○	○		●	●	○	●	●	●	○						
Liverpool	Music	◐	○	○		○	○		○	○	○	○						
	Popular music ①									○	○	○						
Liverpool Hope	Music ①	○	○	○		○	○	○	○	○	○	○						
LIPA	Music	●	○	○	●	○	●	○		○	●	●	○		●		●	●
	Performing arts (music) ①	●	●	●	○	○	○	○		○	○	○	○				○	○
	Sound technology									○	○	○	●	●		●	●	●
Liverpool John Moores	Popular music studies											●						●
Manchester	Music ①	◐	◐	◐		◐	○	○	●	●	○	○		○	○			
Manchester Metropolitan	Music	○	○	○		○	○	○		●	○	○						
Middlesex	Jazz ①	◐			●	○	●	○	●	○	○							
	Music	●	○	○	○	○	○	○		○	●	○						
Napier	Music	●	●				○	○	●	○	○							
Newcastle	Folk and traditional music	●	○	●	○	○	●	○	●	○	○		○	○	○	○	○	○
	Music	○	○	○	○	○	○	○	◐	◐	○	○	○	○	○	○	○	○
Newcastle C	Popular, jazz and commercial music ①	◐	◐	○			◐		●	○		○						
Nottingham	Music	○	○						●	○	○	○						
Oxford	Music	○	○						◐	○	○							
Oxford Brookes	Music ①	○	○	○		○	○	○	○	●	●							
Portsmouth	Music and sound technology ①	○	○	○	○	○	◐	○	◐	◐	○	○	◐	○	○	○	◐	◐
Roehampton	Music	●	○	●		○	○	○	○	○	○							
Royal Academy of Music	Music ①	●	●	○	○	●	●	●	○	●	●	●						
Royal C Music	Music	●	○	●		◐	○	○	●	●	○	○						
Royal Holloway	Music	◐	○	○		○	○	○	◐	◐	○	○		○	○			○
Royal N C Music	Performance/composition	●	●			●	●		○	○	○							
Royal Scottish A Music & Drama	Music	●	●	○		●	●	○	●	○	●	○						
	Scottish music	●	●				●			○	●						○	○
	Scottish music (piping)	●	●				●			○	●						○	○
Royal Welsh C Music & Drama	Music ①	○	○	○		○	●	○	●	○	●	○						

Music

Course content: performance, composition and production

Legend: ① ②: see notes after table — ○ optional; ● compulsory; ◐ compulsory + options

Institution	Course title	Solo instrument	Solo singing	Choir	Improvisation	Orchestra	Small ensemble	Conducting	Imitative exercises	Original work	Orchestration	Electronic music	Popular music	Classical music	Electronic music	Multimedia	Live music	Studio production
Salford	Popular music and recording ①	●			○	●	○			●	●	●						
Sheffield	Music ①	◐	○	○		○	○		◐	○	○	○						
	Traditional music with folklore studies	◐	○	○		○	○		◐	○	○	○						
SOAS	Music studies	○						●										
Southampton	Music	◐	○			○	◐		●	○	○	○						
Staffordshire	Music technology								○	○	○	○	●	○	○	●	●	●
Strathclyde	Applied music ①	●	○	●		○	●	○	○	●	○							
Surrey	Music ①	○	○	◐		◐	○	◐	◐	○	◐	○						
	Music and sound recording (Tonmeister) ②	○	○	○		○	○		◐	○	◐	○	◐	◐	◐	◐	◐	○
	Music with computer sound design	○	○	○	○	○	○	○		◐	○	◐		○	○	●	○	
Sussex	Music ①	○	○	◐		◐	○		●	●	○							
Swansea IHE	Music technology												●		●	●	●	●
Trinity C Music	Music	●	●	◐		◐	◐	○	○	○	○							
Ulster	Music	●	●	●		○	○	○	●	●	●	●						
Westminster	Commercial music	○				●				●		●	●				○	○	●
Wolverhampton	Music ①	●	◐	◐		◐	○	◐	○	●	●	○						
	Popular music ②	●	○	◐		○	○		○	●	●							
York	Music ①	◐	○	◐		◐	○	◐	◐	◐	◐	○						
York St John	Performance: music	○	○	○		◐	●	●	○	●	●	●						

Anglia Ruskin ①Music and technology; piano accompaniment
Bangor ①Music in the community
Bath Spa ①Keyboard skills/elementary keyboard; aural training
Birmingham ①Musical theatre; keyboard
Central Lancashire ①Voice; experimental composition
City ①N Indian classical music; African drumming; Gamelan
Glasgow ①Free composition
Goldsmiths ①Songwriting
Hertfordshire ①Studio techniques ②③Performing with School's gong-chime orchestra; fieldwork and workshops
Huddersfield ①Sound recording
Hull ①Audio recording; film composition ②Pscyhoacoustics and studio design; interactive technology; digital signal processing
Keele ①Multi-speaker live diffusion
King's College London ①General musicianship
Leeds ①Practical skills (ensemble performance plus aural perception skills)
Liverpool ①Composition for moving image
Liverpool Hope ①Keyboard musicianship
LIPA ①Songwriting; composition for film and TV; sound recording; MIDI technology; music production

Manchester ①Musicianship skills
Middlesex ①Arrangement; transcription
Newcastle C ①Musical direction; arranging; improvisation
Oxford Brookes ①Big band; rock bands
Portsmouth ①Radio; music software
Royal Academy of Music ①Repertoire and performance practice; keyboard skills; aural
Royal Welsh C Music & Drama ①Aural training; keyboard musicianship; chamber music
Salford ①Group improvisation; studio production; music video; aural perception
Sheffield ①Piano accompaniment
Strathclyde ①Music workshopping; improvisation; rhythmic skills; drum kit; keyboard skills; guitar; recording and sound production
Surrey ①Keyboard skills compulsory (year 1) ②Audio laboratory; electronics laboratory; location recording
Sussex ①Aural/keyboard skills
Wolverhampton ①Multi-track/computer composition ②Popular music composition and performance
York ①Music theatre production; aural training; gamelan; jazz

Music

Analytical work Analysis of the music of earlier periods and of techniques of composition, form and style has always been fundamental to music study. Analysis of the music of the contemporary period is now an important part (and sometimes the core) of programmes – this can include popular music and the music of non-Western cultures. In the last 20 years, with the advent of computerised technology, there has been a huge growth in the study of how sound is made and shaped, encoded and decoded. Courses tend to fall into one of two categories: those that look to the past for their identity, and those that look to the ever-developing technologies of the future. Both kinds can be academically rigorous, and both can produce fine musical minds amongst the next generation. You must ask yourself where you would feel most at home.

Contextual work A systematic study of the history of Western music and its composers used to be an integral part of almost every degree programme. It is still frequently found, and often in some depth, but on many programmes it is complemented by study of the critical and social contexts for music. Assessments in the earlier years normally require a general knowledge of the outlines of Western music history. General courses in music history seldom begin earlier than the sixteenth century, and 1900 is often used as a convenient dividing point in the syllabus. In the later stages, you may have the option of studying a particular historical period in detail, or of focusing on the contexts provided by disciplines like ethnomusicology, feminism, or cultural studies.

TABLE 3b gives information about the topics other than practical performance that feature in individual courses.

Table 3b — Course content: theoretical work

O optional; ● compulsory; ◐ compulsory + options

Institution	Course title	Study of set works	Analysis	Criticism	Historical musicology	Culture and society	Acoustics	Early music/notation	20th-century music	Ethnomusicology	Popular music	Jazz	Music for the moving image	Others
Anglia Ruskin	Audio and music technology						●				O	O	O	
	Music	◐	◐	●				O	O	O	O	O		Music therapy; instrumental teaching; school music teaching
Bangor	Music	O	O	O	◐			O	O	O	O	O	O	Welsh music; tonal studies; music in society
Bath Spa	Creative music technology	●		●	●	●		●					●	
	Music	◐	O	◐				O	◐	◐	O	O	O	Music technology; music in action
Belfast	Ethnomusicology									●				History, theory, methods and practice in ethnomusicology
	Music	●	◐	O			O	O	●	O				Music in worship; psychology of music; musical instruments
Birmingham	Music	O	●	O		O		●	●	O	●	O		Recording; composers and musicians; cultural theory
Brighton	Digital music	●	●	O		O	O	●		◐			●	Sound art; music for the internet
	Music and visual art		●	●		◐	◐		◐	O	◐		●	

Music

Course content: theoretical work

Key: ○ optional; ● compulsory; ◐ compulsory + options

Institution	Course title	Study of set works	Analysis	Criticism	Historical musicology	Culture and society	Acoustics	Early music/notation	20th-century music	Ethnomusicology	Popular music	Jazz	Music for the moving image	Others
Bristol	Music		◐	○				○	●	○	○	○		Aesthetics
Brunel	Creative music technology	●	●	●	●	●	●		●	○	○	○	○	
	Music	●	●	●	●	●			●	○	○	○		
Cambridge	Music	●	●	○			●	●	●	◐	◐			
Canterbury CC	Music		○	○						○		○		
Cardiff	*Both courses*	○	●	○				○	○	○		○	○	
Central Lancashire	Music practice		○	○		○	○		○	○	○	○	○	
Chester	Popular music		●	●		●					●	●		
Chichester	Music	◐	◐	◐	◐			○		◐	◐	◐	○	Music theatre; opera
	Music with instrumental/vocal teaching	●	●	●	●	◐	○	○	○	○	○	○	○	
City	Music	◐	◐				○	○	●	●		◐	○	Music therapy; music technology; sound recording
Colchester I	Music		○	○				○	○	○	○	○		Music history
Coventry	Music and professional practice	●	●	●					●		○	○		Music technology; theory and aural
	Music composition and professional practice	●	●	●					●	○	○		●	Music technology; theory and aural
Dartington CA	Music	◐	◐	◐			◐		◐	◐	◐	◐		Options in music (performance) and music (composition) through modular choice from year 2
De Montfort	Music technology and innovation	●	●	●	●	●	●		●	○			●	
Derby	Popular music (production)		○	○					○		○	○		
Durham	Music	●	●	●	●	●	○	●	●	●	○	○		
East Anglia	Music	○	○	○					○	○		○	○	
Edinburgh	History of art and history of music	○	○	○				○	○	○	○			Palaeography; notation; musical method; history of instruments; aesthetics
	Music	◐	◐	◐				◐	◐	◐	◐		◐	
Glasgow	*Both courses*		●	●	●	●	●	○	○	○	○	○		Musicianship; musical techniques
Goldsmiths	Music	◐	◐	◐				○	●	○	○	○		Music technology
	Popular music studies		●	○		●			◐	○	●	●	○	Music industry/business; politics of music/sound
Grimsby IFHE	Creative music and digital media studies	◐	●	●	◐		●	◐	◐	●	◐	◐	◐	
Guildhall S Music & Drama	Music	●	●	●					●	●	○		●	
Hertfordshire	Electronic music	●	●	○			●		●			○	○	
Huddersfield	Music	◐	●	●				○	○	●	○	○	○	Study skills
Hull	Creative music technology	●	●	●				○	●					
	Music	○	○	○		○		○	○		○	○	○	Psychology of music; creative music technology
Keele	Music	●	◐	●			○	●	●	◐	○	○		
	Music technology	●	◐	●			○		●		◐		●	
King's College London	Music	○	◐	○				○	◐	○				History of music
Kingston	Creative music technologies		●	○	○	○	●		●	○	○	○	○	
	Music		◐	○	○	○	◐		●	○	○	○		
	Music composition		●	○	○	○	○		●	○	○	○		
	Music performance		●	○	○	○	○		○	○	○	○		

(continued) Table 3b

Course content: theoretical work

Legend: ○ optional; ● compulsory; ◐ compulsory + options

Institution	Course title	Study of set works	Analysis	Criticism	Historical musicology	Culture and society	Acoustics	Early music/notation	20th-century music	Ethnomusicology	Popular music	Jazz	Music for the moving image	Others
Kingston (continued)	Popular musics		●	○	○		●	○		●	●	●	○	
Leeds	Music	●	●	○					○	◐	○	○	○	Music technology
	Popular and world musics	○	◐	◐			◐	○	○	◐	◐	○		Technology/science of music
Leeds C Music	Jazz studies	●	●	●			○		●	○	●	●		
	Music	●	●	●			○		●	○	○			
Liverpool	Music			○	○	○	○	○	●		○	○	○	
	Popular music				●						●	●		Music business; film and TV music; music and society
Liverpool Hope	Music		●	●					●	○	○	○		Electro-acoustic studies; music therapy; work-based learning
LIPA	Music								●		●	○	○	
	Performing arts (music)	●	●								●	○	○	
	Sound technology		●			●					●			
Liverpool John Moores	Popular music studies		●	●		●			●		●			
Manchester	Music	●	●		○	○	○	○	◐	◐	○			
Manchester Metropolitan	Music	○	●	●				●	●	○	○	○		
Middlesex	Jazz	●	●									●		
	Music	●	●	●	●	○	○		●	○	○	○		
Napier	Music	●	●						●			○		
Newcastle	Folk and traditional music	○	●	◐	◐	◐	●	○	○	●	●	●	○	○
	Music	●	◐	◐	◐	◐	●	◐	●	●	●	◐	○	○
Newcastle C	Popular, jazz and commercial music	●	●	●							●	●		Music technology
Nottingham	Music	○	○	○					○	◐	●		○	
Oxford	Music		◐	○				○	◐	◐				
Oxford Brookes	Music	●	●	○					○	○		○	○	Musicology; opera and politics; music in society
Portsmouth	Music and sound technology			○	◐	○	○	◐		◐	○	◐	○	◐
Roehampton	Music	○	◐	◐				○	○	○	○		○	Harmony; music theory
Royal Academy of Music	Music	●	●	○	○	○	○	○	●	○	○	○		
Royal C Music	Music	●	●	○				○	○	●	○		○	
Royal Holloway	Music	◐	◐	○	◐	◐			◐	◐	◐	○		○ · Music in social/political/cultural/geographical context
Royal N C Music	Performance/composition	○	○	○				○	○	◐		○	○	
Royal Scottish A Music & Drama	Music	●	●					○	●	○		○		
	Scottish music	●	●						●	●				
	Scottish music (piping)	●	●						●	●				
Royal Welsh C Music & Drama	Music	●	●	○				○	◐	◐	◐		○	Music therapy; organology; comparative arts; music technology; Welsh music; Baroque performance practice; music in Christian worship; community music
Salford	Popular music and recording	●	●	●			○		○		●	○		African popular music; Latin American percussion; transcription; business and professional practice
Sheffield	Music	●	◐	○				○	○		○	○		Psychology of music; historical performance practice; music therapy

Course content: theoretical work

Key: ○ optional; ● compulsory; ◐ compulsory + options

Institution	Course title	Study of set works	Analysis	Criticism	Historical musicology	Culture and society	Acoustics	Early music/notation	20th-century music	Ethnomusicology	Popular music	Jazz	Music for the moving image	Others
Sheffield (continued)	Traditional music with folklore studies	●	◐	○				○	○		○	○		
SOAS	Music studies	●						○	○	●				Transcription; Asian, African and Middle Eastern music
Southampton	Music	◐	○	○			○	○	●	○	○	○	○	History/analysis of recorded music
Staffordshire	Music technology	●			○		●	○	○		○	○		
Strathclyde	Applied music	○	●					○	○	●	●	●	●	Music in cultural/social contexts; music technology
Surrey	Music	○	◐	○	○	◐	◐	○	◐	◐	○	◐	◐	Study skills; knowledge of instruments; arts policy and practice; music technology; music management
	Music and sound recording (Tonmeister)	○	○	○		◐	●	◐	○	○	○	○		Electroacoustics; acoustics; mathematics; electronics; recording techniques; recording portfolio; audio engineering; audio research; video engineering; audio signal processing; computer audio; sound synthesis; score studies
	Music with computer sound design	○	○	○	○	○	◐	●	○	●	○	●	●	Music technology; music industry; popular music harmony; dance music; synthesis and sampling; creating music with computers; study skills
Sussex	Music	●	●	○				●		○				Aesthetics and sociology
Swansea IHE	Music technology				●	●				●				
Thames Valley	Music (performance/composition)							●			●	●		
	Popular music performance							●			●	●		
Trinity C Music	Music	●	●	○				○	●			○		Harmony and counterpoint; special history periods
Ulster	Music	●	●	●				●	●		○	○		
Westminster	Commercial music	●	○	●				●	●	●	●	○	●	Music business; music sociology and cultural criticism; music law; music journalism
Wolverhampton	Music	○	●	●				○	○	○	○	○		Music therapy
	Popular music	○	◐	◐				○	○	○	●	●		
York	Music		●	●				○	○	◐	○	○		
York St John	Performance: music	●	●	●				○	○	●	●	○	○	

Additional or contextual subjects Most courses involve the study of one or more additional or subsidiary subjects outside music. There are differences in the number of these subjects that the student is expected to study, the length of time over which they are studied and the choice available. TABLE 3c gives some basic information, and the final column shows whether you can select one or more additional subjects from a wide range of more than 20, as is often the case in modular schemes. Details of combined courses in which the second subject forms at least a third of the degree course are given in TABLE 2b.

Additional subjects

Institution	Course title	English	Fine art	History of art	Latin	Philosophy	History	Languages	Mathematics	Electronics	Choice from more than 20
Anglia Ruskin	Audio and music technology	●						●	●	●	
	Music	●	●	●		●	●	●	●	●	●
Bangor	Music	●					●	●	●	●	●
Bath Spa	Music	●	●								
Belfast	Music	●			●	●	●	●	●		●
Birmingham	Music	●		●	●	●	●	●			
Brighton	Music and visual art		●	●							
Bristol	Music	●		●		●		●			●
Brunel	Music	●		●			●	●			
Cardiff	Music	●				●	●	●			●
	Music (BMus)							●			
Chichester	Music	●	●				●		●		
Coventry	Music technology								●	●	
Dartington CA	Music		●								
Derby	Popular music (production)										●
Durham	Music	●			●	●	●	●	●		
East Anglia	Music										●
Glasgow	Music (MA)	●	●	●	●	●	●	●			●
Goldsmiths	Music	●		●			●	●			
Huddersfield	Music	●						●			
Hull	Creative music technology	●	●				●				
	Music	●				●	●	●			●
Keele	Both courses										●
King's College London	Music			●				●			
Kingston	Music							●			
Lancaster	Musicology										●
Leeds	Music	●	●	●			●	●	●	●	
	Popular and world musics										●
Liverpool	Music										●
Liverpool Hope	Music	●	●				●	●	●		
Manchester	Music										●
Manchester Metropolitan	Music										●
Middlesex	Both courses										●
Napier	Music										●
Newcastle	Folk and traditional music	●	●	●	●		●	●	●	●	●
	Music	●	●	●	●	●	●	●	●	●	●
Nottingham	Music	●	●	●	●	●	●	●	●	●	●
Oxford Brookes	Music										●
Portsmouth	Music and sound technology							●			
Roehampton	Music				●			●			
Royal Academy of Music	Music	●	●	●		●	●	●		●	●
Royal C Music	Music	●					●	●	●	●	
Royal Holloway	Music	●			●		●	●	●		
Royal N C Music	Performance/composition							●			
Sheffield	Music	●				●	●	●			●
SOAS	Music studies			●			●	●			●

Music

27

Additional subjects

Institution	Course title	English	Fine art	History of art	Latin	Philosophy	History	Languages	Mathematics	Electronics	Choice from more than 20
Southampton	Music		●	●		●	●	●	●		●
Staffordshire	Music technology							●	●	●	
Surrey	All courses	●						●			
Sussex	Music										●
Trinity C Music	Music							●			
Westminster	Commercial music						●	●			●
York	Music	●	●	●		●	●	●	●	●	●
York St John	Performance: music	●						●			

Teaching methods The non-practical components of most courses are taught using a mixture of lectures, individual or group tutorials, and seminars (larger discussion groups). The balance between these varies from one institution to another and often between the early and late stages of a course, where the emphasis may switch from lectures to smaller group teaching.

Instrumental tuition This is still one of the cornerstones of many courses. Much of the teaching is on a one-to-one basis and many courses attract as teachers gifted professional musicians who see this kind of work as very important. Sometimes a college or university will have a resident ensemble, composer or soloist whose commitment will include some teaching. The opportunities such contacts open up to the student are invaluable. On the downside, it is often the case nowadays that individual tuition has to be paid for by the student, so you need to be prepared to budget for such expenditure.

Assessment methods Most institutions use a variety of assessment methods such as formal written examinations, continuous assessment of coursework and extended projects or dissertations. TABLE 4 gives information about the balance between these methods. It shows in which years there are written examinations and if they contribute to the final degree classification. However, the contribution from examinations in earlier years is often less than the contribution from the examinations in the final year. You should also note that although an examination may not contribute to the final result, passing it may be a condition for continuing with the course.

Many courses allow a wide range of options, which are often assessed in different ways, so it is difficult to give precise figures for the contributions of different assessment methods. For this reason, TABLE 4 shows the possible maximum and minimum contributions from coursework and projects or dissertations.

Projects Project work plays an important part in the assessment of many courses. Projects are usually carried out in the final year and give you the opportunity to pursue particular interests in greater depth, and bring together a range of knowledge and skills learnt during the course.

Students often find projects the most interesting and involving part of the course, though they can also be one of the most challenging.

Portfolios Work in composition or sound recording is often assessed via a portfolio at the end of a year. This will consist of a varied selection of work undertaken during the year and often means that you can work more at your own pace.

Music

29

Frequency of assessment   On many types of course, especially modular courses, assessment is carried out more frequently than in the traditional pattern of end-of-year examinations. Often, each module is assessed independently, soon after it has been completed. The precise details of when assessments are carried out vary from course to course: TABLE 4 shows if courses are assessed every term, semester (there are two semesters in a year) or year. Note that in modular courses, even if all modules are assessed, those occurring early in the course may not contribute as much to the final result as those later in the course.

The mix of assessment methods   All assessment systems have advantages and disadvantages: for example, reducing the significance of final examinations may simply mean that short periods of high stress are replaced by a series of deadlines and continuous low-level stress throughout the course. Which of these you prefer will depend on your temperament. Because students vary in their response to different assessment methods, institutions usually employ a combination of methods, which also allows them to match the assessment method to the skill being tested. In some cases you may be able to change the make-up of your assessment regime, for example by choosing a dissertation or project instead of a formal examination.

Table 4 — Assessment methods

Institution	Course title	Frequency of assessment	Performance assessment	Portfolio assessment (●=yes)	Years of exams contributing to final degree (years of exams not contributing to final degree)	Coursework: minimum/maximum %	Project/dissertation: minimum/maximum %
Anglia Ruskin	Audio and music technology	◐			(1),2,3	40/60	11/11
	Music	◐	◐		(1),2,3	50/65	12/12
Bangor	Music	◐	◐	●	(1)	55/88	12/45
Bath Spa	Creative music technology	◐		●	(1)	50/50	30/50
	Music	◐	◐		(1)	73/91	0/9
Belfast	Ethnomusicology	◐	◐		1,2,3	13/13	20/30
	Music	◐	◐		1,2,3	33/67	0/17
Birmingham	Music	◐	◐		(1),2,3	15/45	15/30
Brighton	Digital music	◑	◑			20/30	70/80
	Music and visual art	◑	◑	●	1,(2),3	20/40	60/80
Bristol	Music	◐	◐		(1)	15/50	25/60
Brunel	Creative music technology	◑			(1),2,3	40/18	18/18
	Music	◑	◑		(1),2,3	40/50	12/23
Cambridge	Music	○	○		(1),(2),3		0/33
Canterbury CC	Music	○	◑		(1),2,3	50	
Cardiff	Both courses	◐	○		(1),2,3	50/60	20/40
Central Lancashire	Music practice	◐	◐	●		80/80	20/20
Chester	Popular music		◐		(1),(2),(3)	50/50	50/50
Chichester	Music	◐	◐		(1),2,3	75	15
	Music with instrumental/vocal teaching	◐	◐		(1),2,3		
City	Music	◑	◑		(1),2,3		60
Colchester I	Music	◐	◐		(1),2,3	50/90	10/50

Key for frequency of assessment and performance assessment columns: ● term; ◐ semester; ○ year

Assessment methods

Institution	Course title	Key for frequency of assessment and performance assessment columns: ◑ semester; ● term; ○ year	Frequency of assessment	Performance assessment	Portfolio assessment (●=yes)	Years of exams contributing to final degree (●) (years of exams not contributing to final degree)	Coursework: minimum/maximum %	Project/dissertation: minimum/maximum %
Coventry	Music and professional practice		◑	◑			80/**80**	20/**20**
	Music composition and professional practice		◑	◑			80/**80**	20/**20**
	Music technology		◑			(1),**2,3**	30/**40**	30/**45**
Dartington CA	Music		◑	○				
De Montfort	Music technology and innovation		○	○			50/**75**	12/**25**
Derby	Popular music (production)		◑	◑		(1),**2,3**	25/**75**	25/**75**
Durham	Music		○		●	(1),**2,3**	40/**60**	40/**60**
East Anglia	Music		○	◑		(1),**2,3**	50/**50**	16/**16**
Edinburgh	History of art and history of music		◑	○		(1),(2),**3,4**	25/**25**	12/**12**
	Music		◑			**1,2,3,4**	0/**100**	0/**100**
	Music technology					(1),(2),**3,4**		
Glasgow	Music (BMus)		◑	◑	●		60/**84**	16/**40**
	Music (MA)		◑	◑	●		70/**90**	10/**30**
Goldsmiths	*Both courses*		◑	◑		**1,2,3**	30/**40**	11/**22**
Grimsby IFHE	Creative music and digital media studies		◑	◑		**2,3**	20/**40**	40/**80**
Guildhall S Music & Drama	Music		◑	●		**1,2,3**		30/**60**
Hertfordshire	Electronic music		◑			(1),**2,3**	50/**70**	30/**50**
Huddersfield	Music		◑	◑		**2,3**	50/**50**	50/**50**
Hull	Creative music technology		◑	◑		(1),**2,3**		25/**25**
	Music		◑	◑	●	(1),**2,3**	0/**33**	33/**66**
	Music technology and computing			○		(1),**2,3**	40/**40**	25/**25**
Keele	Music		◑	◑		**3**	50/**66**	17/**50**
	Music technology		◑		●	**3**	8/**12**	90/**92**
King's College London	Music		◑	○		**1,2,3**	50/**50**	20/**50**
Kingston	Creative music technologies		◑		●		40	60
	Music		◑		●		60	40
	Music composition		◑		●		40	60
	Music performance		◑	◑	●		60	40
	Popular musics		◑		●		40	60
Leeds	Music		◑	◑		(1),**2,3,4**	60/**80**	20/**40**
	Popular and world musics		◑	◑		**1,2,3**		40/**90**
Leeds C Music	Jazz studies		◑	◑		(1),**2,3**		
	Music		◑			(1),**2,3**		
Liverpool	Music		◑	○		(1),**2,3**	54/**79**	20/**40**
	Popular music		◑			(1),**2**	50/**80**	20/**50**
Liverpool Hope	Music		○	○		**2,3**	10/**45**	0/**40**
LIPA	Music		◑	◑	●	**2**	20	80
	Performing arts (music)		◑	◑	●		20	80
	Sound technology		◑			(1),**2**	30/**30**	60/**70**
Liverpool John Moores	Popular music studies		◑			(1),**2,3**		
Manchester	Music		◑	○	●	(1),**2,3**	33/**66**	20/**33**
Manchester Metropolitan	Music		◑	◑			40/**70**	30/**60**
Middlesex	Jazz		◑	○	●	(1),**2,3**	60/**100**	0/**40**
	Music		◑	○	●	**1,2**	60/**100**	0/**40**
Napier	Music		◑	◑				

Music

31

Music

Assessment methods

Institution	Course title	Key for frequency of assessment and performance assessment columns: ◑ term; ○ semester; ○ year	Frequency of assessment	Performance assessment	Portfolio assessment (●=yes)	Years of exams contributing to final degree (years of exams not contributing to final degree)	Coursework: minimum/maximum %	Project/dissertation: minimum/maximum %
Newcastle	Folk and traditional music		◑	○	●	(1),(2),**3,4**	60/**80**	20/**40**
	Music		◑	◑	●	(1),**2,3,4**	70/**78**	22/**30**
Newcastle C	Popular, jazz and commercial music		◑	◑		(1),**2**	**50**	**50**
Nottingham	Music		◑	◑		(1),**2,3**	**50**	**40**
Oxford	Music		○	○		(1),**3**	0/**50**	0/**50**
Oxford Brookes	Music		◑				50/**88**	12/**12**
Portsmouth	Music and sound technology		◑	○		(1),**2,3**	70/**75**	20/**25**
Roehampton	Music		◑	◑		(1),**2,3**	50/**50**	20/**20**
Rose Bruford C	Actor-musician		◐	◐				
Royal Academy of Music	Music		◐	◐	●	**1,2,3,4**	30/**50**	15/**20**
Royal C Music	Music		○	○		(1),**2**	**20**	10/**70**
Royal Holloway	Music		◐	○	●	(1),**2,3**	30/**50**	10/**10**
Royal N C Music	Performance/composition		○	○		**1,2,4**		
Royal Scottish A Music & Drama	Music		◐	◐		(1),(2),(3),(4)		
	Scottish music		◐	◐				
	Scottish music (piping)		◐	◐				
Royal Welsh C Music & Drama	Music		○	○		(1),**2,3**	30/**35**	20/**20**
Salford	Popular music and recording		◑	◑		(1),**2**	20/**25**	40/**75**
Sheffield	*Both courses*		◑	○		(1)	20/**40**	50/**80**
SOAS	Music studies		○	○		(1),**2,3**	20/**30**	0/**10**
Southampton	Music		◑	◑		(1),**2,3**	40/**100**	0/**31**
Staffordshire	Music technology		◑	○		(1),**2,3**	30/**50**	35/**40**
Strathclyde	Applied music		◑	◑		(1),(2),**3,4**	25/**30**	25/**60**
Surrey	Music		◑	◑	●	(1),**2,3,4**	33/**40**	25/**33**
	Music and sound recording (Tonmeister)		◑	◑	●	(1),**2,3,4**	20/**40**	30/**30**
	Music with computer sound design		◑	◑	●	(1),**2,3**	33/**40**	25/**33**
Sussex	Music		○	○		(1),**2,3**	0/**15**	0/**25**
Swansea IHE	Music technology		◑			(1),**2,3**	40	40
Thames Valley	Music (performance/composition)		◑	◑				
	Popular music performance		◑	◑				
Trinity C Music	Music		◑	◑			25/**75**	25/**75**
Ulster	Music		◑	◑		(1),**2,3**	49/**68**	12/**12**
Westminster	Commercial music		◐	◐	●	(1),**2,3**		50/**60**
Wolverhampton	Music		◑	◑		(1),**2,3**	75	**12**
	Popular music		◑	◑		(1),**2,3**	87	**12**
York	Music		○	○			0/**10**	60/**100**
York St John	Performance: music		◑	◑			50/**50**	50/**50**

How to apply   With some exceptions (see below), applications for courses in this Guide must be made online at www.ucas.com, the website of the Universities and Colleges Admissions Service (UCAS).

For performance-based courses at Birmingham Conservatoire, Leeds C Music, Royal C Music, Royal N C Music, Royal Scottish A Music & Drama, Royal Welsh C Music & Drama and Trinity C Music applications must be made online through the Conservatoires UK Admissions Service, www.cukas.ac.uk (also accessible from the UCAS website).

The UCAS tariff   The UCAS points scheme, or 'tariff', combines GCE Advanced levels, GCE Advanced Subsidiary levels, AVCE and Scottish qualifications in a single points system. For example, a GCE A-level with an A grade or a Scottish Advanced Higher with an A grade will score 120 points, while an AS-level with an A grade, an A-level with a D grade, or a Scottish Higher with a B grade will score 60 points.

For some courses, entrance requirements are expressed simply in terms of points, but many also make offers in terms of particular grades in A-levels or Highers, and some require minimum grades in specific A-levels or Highers. TABLE 5 summarises these requirements. However, for many courses the requirements are more complex, so you should take the information in the table only as a starting point, and an indication of the relative demands of the courses. It is vital to check prospectuses and university and college websites, to find out the full details of requirements for any courses you are considering.

Evidence of ability in performance   For music courses in which performance plays an important part, you are likely to have to give some evidence of your abilities, whether in the form of passes in grade examinations, an audition, or both. TABLE 5 indicates where this is the case.

Other qualifications   All institutions accept certain other qualifications for their general requirement. For example, the International Baccalaureate (IB) and the European Baccalaureate (EB) are generally accepted. The publications listed in Chapter 6 give information about some other qualifications and about the acceptability of the IB and the EB for course-specific requirements. Again, if in doubt, you should consult institutions direct.

Institutions are becoming increasingly flexible about entrance requirements, so you should not assume that you will not be accepted if you lack standard qualifications. For example, in some franchising schemes you can begin at a level below the starting point of a degree course by taking the early stages of a course at a college of further education. Provided you are successful, you will then move on to an institution of higher education for the later stages of the course. You may also be interested in the Access courses

Music

offered at some universities and colleges, some of which are taught in the evenings. Successful completion of an Access course, while not guaranteeing you a place on a degree course, will give you an advantage when you apply.

Open days and interviews   Many institutions and departments run open days, when you can look round their facilities and meet staff and students. In some cases you may be invited to visit only after you have been offered a place. For some courses, interviews play an important part in the selection process. They are usually conducted in as relaxed and friendly a manner as possible; the intention is to find out more about your personal qualities than can be learned from your application form alone.

Student numbers   TABLE 5 also gives an estimate of the number of students on each course (the figure is shown in brackets if it is the total for a larger group, such as a faculty, or if it includes other students, such as those on a combined degree scheme, not just those studying music). This number will give you some idea of how many other students you are likely to be taught with, but you should remember that some lectures may be common to several courses, and students on the same course may choose different specialised options, particularly in later years.

You should bear in mind that there is no simple equation between the number of places and the probability of acceptance, since a course with a large number of places may have those places because it is popular and oversubscribed. You cannot even use the ratio of applicants to places as a reliable guide, as one course may have relatively few applicants because it is known to have high entrance requirements, while another may attract a large number of applicants who view it as an insurance policy in case they fail to gain entry to another course.

Entrance requirements   The information in TABLE 5 is for general guidance only, since admissions tutors consider applicants individually, and may take many factors into account other than examination grades.

Table 5	Entrance requirements									
Institution	**Course title**	**Number of students** (includes other courses)	**Typical offers**	UCAS tariff points	A-levels	SCQF Highers	**A-level Music** ● compulsory; ○ preferred	**Practical test**	**Grade examinations** ● required; ○ instead of, or ◑ in addition to A-levels	
Anglia Ruskin	Audio and music technology			180		BBCC				
	Music	90		160–180		BBCC			●	◑
Bangor	Music	55		260–280	BBC		●			
Bath Spa	Creative music technology	70		200–240						
	Music	30		200–240			○	●	●	◑
Belfast	Ethnomusicology	40			BBB	BBBBB	○			
	Music	(35)			BBC	BBBBB				
Birmingham	Music	60			AAB	AABBB	●		●	◑

Entrance requirements

Institution	Course title	Number of students (includes other courses)	Typical offers UCAS tariff points	A-levels	SCQF Highers	A-level Music (● compulsory; ○ preferred)	Practical test	Grade examinations (● required; ○ instead of, or ◐ in addition to A-levels)
Brighton	Digital music	25	160	CCC		○		
	Music and visual art	22				○		
Bristol	Music	40		ABB	AAAAB	●		
Brunel	Creative music technology	32	280	BBC	BBBBC	○		● ○
	Music	32	280	BBC	BBBBC	●		● ○
Cambridge	Music	65		AAA		●		
Canterbury CC	Music	50		CC	CCCC	●	●	● ◐
Cardiff	Music	25		BBB	BBBBB	●	●	● ◐
	Music (BMus)	55		BBB	BBBBB	●	●	● ◐
Central Lancashire	Music practice	25	160	CC		○		
Chester	Popular music		240–260	CCC	BBBB	○		
Chichester	Music	50	160–220			○	●	● ○
	Music with instrumental/vocal teaching	50	160–220			●		
City	Music	27	260–300		AABB	●	●	● ◐
Colchester I	Music	40	160		CCCC	○	●	● ◐
Coventry	Music and professional practice	16	200–220			○		
	Music composition and professional practice		200–220					
	Music technology	20	280		BBBB	○		
Dartington CA	Music	50	160–200			○	●	● ◐
De Montfort	Music technology and innovation	60	160–240		BBBB	○		
Derby	Popular music (production)	(25)	140–180			○		
Durham	Music	45		ABC	AAABB	●	●	
East Anglia	Music	25	280			●	●	● ◐
Edinburgh	History of art and history of music			BBB	BBBB	●		
	Music			BBB	ABBC	●		● ◐
	Music technology			BBB	ABBC	●		● ◐
Glasgow	Music (BMus)	16		BBC	BBBB	○	●	● ◐
	Music (MA)	60		ABB	BBBB	○		
Goldsmiths	Music	65		BBB	BBBBB	●	●	● ◐
	Popular music studies	25		BBB	BBBBB	●		
Grimsby IFHE	Creative music and digital media studies	10	120–220			○		
Guildhall S Music & Drama	Music	100				○	●	
Hertfordshire	Electronic music	15	200–240			○		● ○
	Music composition and technology		240–280					
	Music technology		220–260					
	Music, commercial composition and technology		240–280					
Huddersfield	Music	100	300		BBBC	●	●	● ◐
Hull	Creative music technology	60	180–240	BCC		●	●	● ◐
	Music	40	240–300	BCC	BBBBB	●		● ◐
	Music technology and computing	13	200–280	CDD	BBCCC	○		
Keele	Music	30	280–300		BBCC	○		● ○
	Music technology	40	260–320		BBCC			
King's College London	Music	28		AAB	AAAAB	●	●	● ◐

Entrance requirements

Institution	Course title	Number of students (includes other courses)	Typical offers UCAS tariff points	A-levels	SCQF Highers	A-level Music ● compulsory; O preferred	Practical test	Grade examinations ● required; O instead of, or ◑ in addition to A-levels	
Kingston	Creative music technologies	(80)	160	CC		O	●		
	Music	(80)	160	CC		O	●		
	Music composition	(80)	160	CC		O	●		
	Music performance	(80)	160	CC		O	●	●	◑
	Popular musics	(80)	160	CC		O	●		
Lancaster	Music	(33)		BBB	BBBCC				
	Musicology	(33)		BBB	BBBCC	O			
Leeds	Music	43		ABC	AAABB	●	●	●	◑
	Popular and world musics	30		ABC		O			
Leeds C Music	Jazz studies	60	240		CCCC	●	●	●	O
	Music		240		CCCC	●	●	●	O
Liverpool	Music	24	320	BBB	ABBBB	●		●	◑
	Popular music	15	320		ABBBB	O			
Liverpool Hope	Music		220			O		●	O
LIPA	Music	35	260				●		
	Performing arts (music)	20	180			O	●		
	Sound technology	32	260						
Liverpool John Moores	Popular music studies	27	240	CCC	BBCC				
Manchester	Music	55		AAB	AAAAB	●		●	◑
Manchester Metropolitan	Music	20	200		BBB	O	●	●	O
Middlesex	Jazz	30	200–220				●		
	Music	15	160–280			O	●	●	◑
Napier	Music	25	200	BC	ABC	●	●		
Newcastle	Folk and traditional music	25	300	BBB	AAAB	O	●		
	Music	50	320	ABB	AAAB	●		●	◑
Newcastle C	Popular, jazz and commercial music	30	160	CC	CCCC	O	●		
Nottingham	Music	39		AAB	AABB	●			
Oxford	Music	55		AAA	AAAAB	●	●		
Oxford Brookes	Music	17		BDD		O	●	●	O
Portsmouth	Music and sound technology	35	240	BC					
Roehampton	Music	30	180			O	●	●	◑
Rose Bruford C	Actor-musician	15	160–280				●		
Royal Academy of Music	Music	99		BC		●	●	●	◑
Royal C Music	Music	100	120			O	●		
Royal Holloway	Music	(45)	300–320			●		●	◑
Royal N C Music	Performance/composition	400				O	●		
Royal Scottish A Music & Drama	Music	30		EE	CCC	O	●		
	Scottish music	10		EE	CCC	O			
	Scottish music (piping)	4		EE	CCC	O			
Royal Welsh C Music & Drama	Music	100				●	●	●	◑
Salford	Popular music and recording	40	260		BBBBB	O	●	●	O
Sheffield	Music	40		ABC	AABB	●	●	●	◑
	Traditional music with folklore studies	2		BBB	ABBB				
SOAS	Music studies	12	260	BCC	BBCCC	●	●		

Music

36

Entrance requirements

Institution	Course title	Number of students (includes other courses)	Typical offers – UCAS tariff points	A-levels	SCQF Highers	A-level Music (● compulsory; ○ preferred)	Practical test	Grade examinations (● required; ○ instead of, or ◐ in addition to A-levels)
Southampton	Music	45	350	BBB		●	●	● ◐
Staffordshire	Music technology	100	280	CCC	BBB			
Strathclyde	Applied music	45		CC	BBC	○	●	
Surrey	Music	13	280	BBC	ABBB	●	●	● ◐
	Music and sound recording (Tonmeister)	24	340	AAB	AABBB	●	●	● ◐
	Music with computer sound design	30	280	BBC	AABBB	○		
Sussex	Music	10		ABB	ABBBB	○		● ◐
Swansea IHE	Music technology	24	220–340					
Thames Valley	Music		160			●	●	●
	Music (performance/composition)		160			●	●	●
	Popular music performance		120			●	●	●
Trinity C Music	Music	90		EE	CCC	○	●	● ◐
Ulster	Music	25	280			○	●	● ◐
Westminster	Commercial music	58		CC	CCCC		●	
Wolverhampton	Music	50	160–220			○	●	● ○
	Popular music	30	160–220			○	●	● ○
York	Music	35		ABB	AABBB	●	●	● ◐
York St John	Performance: music	20	160		BBC	○	●	● ◐

Music

Publications   Unless indicated otherwise, all items in the following list are available from Trotman Publishing; phone 0870 900 2665, or buy online at www.trotman.co.uk (follow the link to 'Careers Portal', then to 'Your Bookshop').

The Big Guide 2008 UCAS, 2007, £29.50

How to Complete Your UCAS Application 2008 Entry Trotman, 2007, £11.99

Scottish Guide 2008 Entry UCAS, 2007, £14.95

The Ultimate University Ranking Guide C Harris. Trotman, 2004, £14.99

Student Book 2008 K Boehm & J Lees-Spalding. Trotman, 2007, £16.99

Experience Erasmus: The UK Guide Careerscope Publications, 2006, £16.95

Taking a Year Off Margaret Flynn. Trotman, 2002, £11.99

Students' Money Matters 2007 G Thomas. Trotman, 2007, £14.99

Mature Students' Directory Trotman, 2004, £19.99

Disabled Students' Guide to University E Caprez. Trotman, 2004, £21.99

Making the Most of University K van Haeften. Trotman, 2003, £9.99

Careers publications

Careers with an Arts or Humanities Degree P Schofield. Lifetime Publishing, 2006, £10.99

Music Industry Uncovered T Stillam. Trotman, 2004, £11.99

British and International Music Yearbook: The Directory of the Classical Music Industry Rhinegold Publishing, 2006 (32nd edition), £34.95, www.rhinegold.co.uk

Websites

Universities and Colleges Admissions Service www.ucas.com

Higher Education Funding Council for England www.aimhigher.ac.uk

Higher Education and Research Opportunities in the United Kingdom www.hero.ac.uk

Teaching Quality Information www.tqi.ac.uk; the site gives a range of information on courses, such as drop-out rates, student satisfaction ratings and graduate destinations

Student Loans Company www.slc.co.uk

Student Support in Scotland www.student-support-saas.gov.uk

Student Support for Northern Ireland www.education-support.org.uk/students

Erasmus www.erasmus.ac.uk

European Commission Erasmus pages http://ec.europa.eu/; use the A–Z to select Education, then (from the menu) Programmes and Actions, then Erasmus

The European Choice: A Guide to Opportunities for Higher Education in Europe www.eurochoice.org.uk

Prospects Occupational Information (Higher Education Career Services Unit) www.prospects.ac.uk; from the 'Jobs and Work' menu, select 'Explore types of jobs'.

National Bureau for Students with Disabilities www.skill.org.uk

Music

Professional societies and organisations

Arts Marketing Association 7a Clifton Court, Clifton Road, Cambridge CB1 7BN; www.a-m-a.co.uk

British Society for Music Therapy 61 Church Hill Road, East Barnet, Hertfordshire EN4 8SY; www.bsmt.org

Incorporated Society of Musicians 10 Stratford Place, London WC1 1AA; www.ism.org

Music Publishers' Association Ltd 6th Floor, British Music House, 26 Berners Street, London W1T 3LR; www.mpaonline.org.uk

The courses This Guide gives you information to help you narrow down your choice of courses. Your next step is to find out more about the courses that particularly interest you. Prospectuses cover many of the aspects you are most likely to want to know about, but some departments produce their own publications giving more specific details of their courses. University and college websites are listed in TABLE 2a, and can be reached via the UCAS site, www.ucas.com.

You can also write to the contacts listed below.

Aberdeen Student Recruitment and Admissions Service (sras@abdn.ac.uk), University of Aberdeen, Regent Walk, Aberdeen AB24 3FX

Anglia Ruskin Contact Centre (answers@anglia.ac.uk), Anglia Ruskin University, Bishop Hall Lane, Chelmsford CM1 1SQ

Bangor Admissions Secretary (muse01@bangor.ac.uk), School of Music, University of Wales, Bangor, Gwynedd LL57 2DG

Bath Spa Creative music technology Nick Sargent (n.sargent@bathspa.ac.uk), Course Director (Creative Music Technology); Music Professor Roger Heaton (r.heaton@bathspa.ac.uk), Course Director (Music); both at Bath Spa University, Newton Park, Bath BA2 9BN

Bedfordshire Admissions Department (admission@beds.ac.uk), University of Bedfordshire, Park Square, Luton LU1 3JU

Belfast Ethnomusicology Martin Stokes, Department of Social Anthropology, The Queen's University of Belfast, 14 University Square; Music Secretary, School of Music, The Queen's University of Belfast; both at Belfast BT7 1NN

Birmingham Dr Kenneth Hamilton (k.l.hamilton@bham.ac.uk), University of Birmingham, PO Box 363, Birmingham B15 2TT

Brighton Lydia Jones (lj9@brighton.ac.uk), Faculty of Arts and Architecture, University of Brighton, Grand Parade, Brighton BN2 0JY

Bristol Admissions Tutor (w.g.jenkins@bris.ac.uk), Department of Music, University of Bristol, Victoria Rooms, Queen's Road, Bristol BS8 1SA

Bristol UWE Pat Cottrell (admissions.cems@uwe.ac.uk), Faculty of Computing, Engineering and Mathematics, University of the West of England Bristol, Coldharbour Lane, Frenchay, Bristol BS16 1QY

Brunel Dr John Croft (john.croft@brunel.ac.uk), School of Arts, Brunel University, Uxbridge UB8 3PH

Cambridge Cambridge Admissions Office (admissions@cam.ac.uk), University of Cambridge, Fitzwilliam House, 32 Trumpington Street, Cambridge CB2 1QY

Canterbury CC Admissions and Recruitment (admissions@canterbury.ac.uk), Canterbury Christ Church University, Canterbury CT1 1QU

Cardiff Dr D Beard (music-ucasenq@cardiff.ac.uk), Department of Music, Cardiff University, Corbett Road, Cardiff CF1 3EB

Central Lancashire Wayne Carlsen (kcorless@uclan.ac.uk), Admissions Tutor, Music Practice, University of Central Lancashire, Chandle Building, Preston PR1 2HE

Chester Media (commercial music production) Brendan O'Sullivan (b.osullivan@chester.ac.uk), Department of Media, University of Chester, Warrington Campus, Crab Lane, Warrington WA2 0DB; Popular music Ben Broughton (b.broughton@chester.ac.uk), Department of Performing Arts, University of Chester, Parkgate Road, Chester CH1 4BJ

Chichester Ben Hall (b.hall@chi.ac.uk), Head of Music, University of Chichester, Bishop Otter Campus, College Lane, Chichester PO19 6PE

City Undergraduate Admissions Office (ugadmissions@city.ac.uk), City University, Northampton Square, London EC1V 0HB

Colchester I Course Enquiry Line (info@colchester.ac.uk), Colchester Institute, Sheepen Road, Colchester, Essex CO3 3LL

Coventry Recruitment and Admissions Office (info.rao@coventry.ac.uk), Coventry University, Priory Street, Coventry CV1 5FB

Dartington CA Admissions (enquiries@dartington.ac.uk), Dartington College of Arts, Totnes, Devon TQ9 6EJ

De Montfort Promotion and Recruitment Centre (huadmiss@dmu.ac.uk), Faculty of Humanities, De Montfort University, The Gateway, Leicester LE1 9BH

Derby Student Recruitment Unit (enquiries-admissions@derby.ac.uk), University of Derby, Kedleston Road, Derby DE22 1GB

Doncaster C Information and Guidance Centre (he@don.ac.uk), Doncaster College, Waterdale, Doncaster DN1 3EX

Durham Secretary, University Music School, University of Durham, Palace Green, Durham DH1 3RL

East Anglia Admissions Officer (Music) (mus.admiss@uea.ac.uk), University of East Anglia, Music Centre, Norwich NR4 7TJ

East London Student Admissions Office (admiss@uel.ac.uk), University of East London, Docklands Campus, 4–6 University Way, London E16 2RD

Edinburgh Undergraduate Admissions Office (hssug@ed.ac.uk), College of Humanities and Social Science, University of Edinburgh, David Hume Tower, Edinburgh EH8 9JX

Glamorgan Student Enquiry Centre (enquiries@glam.ac.uk), University of Glamorgan, Pontypridd, Mid Glamorgan CF37 1DL

Glasgow Music (BMus) Dr David Lode, BMus Admissions, Music Department, Glasgow University, 14 University Gardens; Music (MA) Faculty Admissions Office, Faculty of Arts, Glasgow University, 6 University Gardens; both at Glasgow G12 8QH

Gloucestershire Admissions (admissions@glos.ac.uk), University of Gloucestershire, Hardwick Campus, St Paul's Road, Cheltenham GL50 4BS

Goldsmiths Admissions Office (admissions@gold.ac.uk), Goldsmiths University of London, New Cross, London SE14 6NW

Grimsby IFHE Higher Education Department (headmissions@grimsby.ac.uk), Grimsby Institute of Further and Higher Education, Nuns Corner, Grimsby, Lincolnshire DN34 5BQ

Guildhall S Music & Drama Registrar (Admissions) (registry@gsmd.ac.uk), Guildhall School of Music & Drama, Barbican, London EC2Y 8DT

TAX INVOICE/RECEIPT
VAT: 208943942

Library: Royal Borough of Windsor and Maidenhead
Branch : CIRCULATION 9
Drawer : MAIDENHEAD LENDING
Receipt: HMAI140555
Staff : MAIDENHEAD LIBRARY
Date : 05/10/2013   Time: 11.41
Brw No : N/A

FRIENDS MERCHANDISE 00.30
VAT 00.00

FRIENDS MERCHANDISE 00.75
VAT 00.00

FRIENDS MERCHANDISE 01.50
VAT 00.00

SUBTOTAL   02.55
ROUNDING   00.00
TOTAL including VAT 02.55

Hertfordshire Electronic music Admissions Tutor (admissions@herts.ac.uk), Faculty of Information Sciences; All other courses Admissions Office (admissions@herts.ac.uk); both at University of Hertfordshire, Hatfield, Hertfordshire AL10 9AB

Huddersfield Michael Holloway (m.l.holloway@hud.ac.uk), Department of Music, University of Huddersfield, Queensgate, Huddersfield HD1 3DH

Hull Creative music technology Scarborough Campus, University of Hull, Filey Road, Scarborough YO11 3AZ; All other courses Dr Elaine King (e.c.king@hull.ac.uk), Department of Music, University of Hull, Hull HU6 7RX

Keele Undergraduate Division (aaa30@keele.ac.uk), Keele University, Staffordshire ST5 5BG

Kent Registry (recruitment@kent.ac.uk), University of Kent, Canterbury, Kent CT2 7NZ

King's College London Ms Jane Elderton (jane.elderton@kcl.ac.uk), Administrator, Department of Music, King's College London, Strand, London WC2R 2LS

Kingston Student Information and Advice Centre, Cooper House, Kingston University, 40–46 Surbiton Road, Kingston upon Thames KT1 2HX

Lancaster Dr Deborah Mawer, Department of Music, Lancaster University, Lancaster LA1 4YW

Leeds Dr Bryan White (b.white@leeds.ac.uk), Tutor for Admissions, Department of Music, University of Leeds, Leeds LS2 9JT

Leeds C Music Admissions Officer (l.dobson@lcm.ac.uk), Leeds College of Music, Cookridge Street, Leeds LS2 8BH

Leeds Metropolitan Course Enquiries (course-enquiries@leedsmet.ac.uk), Leeds Metropolitan University, Civic Quarter, Leeds LS1 3HE

Liverpool Administrator (jastorey@liv.ac.uk), Department of Music, University of Liverpool, 80 Bedford Street South, Liverpool L69 3BX

Liverpool Hope Admissions (admission@hope.ac.uk), Liverpool Hope University, Hope Park, Liverpool L16 9JD

LIPA Admissions (admissions@lipa.ac.uk), Liverpool Institute for Performing Arts, Mount Street, Liverpool L1 9HF

Liverpool John Moores Student Recruitment Team (recruitment@ljmu.ac.uk), Liverpool John Moores University, Roscoe Court, 4 Rodney Street, Liverpool L1 2TZ

London Metropolitan Admissions Office (admissions@londonmet.ac.uk), London Metropolitan University, 166–220 Holloway Road, London N7 8DB

Manchester Undergraduate Recruitment and Admissions Office, University of Manchester, Oxford Road, Manchester M13 9PL

Manchester Metropolitan Graham Shrubsole (g.shrubsole@mmu.ac.uk), Course Leader BA Joint Honours (Arts), Manchester Metropolitan University, Alsager, Cheshire ST7 2HL

Middlesex Admissions Enquiries (admissions@mdx.ac.uk), Middlesex University, North London Business Park, Oakleigh Road South, London N11 1QS

Napier Information Office (info@napier.ac.uk), Napier University, 10 Colinton Road, Edinburgh EH14 5DT

Newcastle Folk and traditional music Jo Goatman (music.ugadmin@ncl.ac.uk), Folk Degree, University of Newcastle upon Tyne, The Sage, St Mary's Square, Gateshead Quays NE8 2JR; Music Secretary (music.ugadmin@ncl.ac.uk), Department of Music, University of Newcastle upon Tyne, Newcastle upon Tyne NE1 7RU

Newcastle C Armstrong Building (james.birkett@ncl-coll.ac.uk), Newcastle College, Rye Hill Campus, Scotswood Road, Newcastle upon Tyne NE4 5BR

Northampton Admissions Office (admissions@northampton.ac.uk), University of Northampton, Park Campus, Broughton Green Road, Northampton NN2 7AL

Northbrook C Admissions Office (enquiries@nbcol.ac.uk), Northbrook College Sussex, Littlehampton Road, Goring by Sea, Worthing BN12 6NU

Nottingham Mrs S Britten (sally.britten@nottingham.ac.uk), Department of Music, University of Nottingham, University Park, Nottingham NG7 2RD

Oxford Oxford Colleges Admissions Office, Oxford University, University Offices, Wellington Square, Oxford OX1 2JD

Oxford Brookes Glenn Archibald (garchibald@brookes.ac.uk), School of Art, Publishing and Music, Oxford Brookes University, Headington, Oxford OX3 0BP

Paisley Assistant Registrar, University of Paisley, High Street, Paisley PA1 2BE

Plymouth Admissions, Faculty of Arts and Education, University of Plymouth, Earl Richards Road North, Exeter EX2 6AS

Portsmouth Ms Emma Newcombe (technology.admissions@port.ac.uk), Admissions Manager, Faculty of Technology, University of Portsmouth, Lion Gate Building, Lion Terrace, Portsmouth PO1 3HF

Roehampton Enquiries Office (enquiries@roehampton.ac.uk), Roehampton University, Roehampton Lane, London SW15 5PU

Rose Bruford C Admissions Office (enquiries@bruford.ac.uk), Rose Bruford College, Lamorbey Park, Sidcup, Kent DA15 9DF

Royal Academy of Music Registry (registry@ram.ac.uk), Royal Academy of Music, Marylebone Road, London NW1 5HT

Royal C Music Publicity Officer, Royal College of Music, Prince Consort Road, London SW7 2BS

Royal Holloway Dr Julie Brown, Admissions Tutor, Royal Holloway, University of London, Egham, Surrey TW20 0EX

Royal N C Music Academic Registrar, Royal Northern College of Music, 124 Oxford Road, Manchester M13 9RD

Royal Scottish A Music & Drama Assistant Registrar (registry@rsamd.ac.uk), Royal Scottish Academy of Music and Drama, 100 Renfrew Street, Glasgow G2 3DB

Royal Welsh C Music & Drama Music Admissions Officer (music.admissions@rwcmd.ac.uk), Royal Welsh College of Music and Drama, Cathays Park, Cardiff CF10 3ER

Salford Roy Humphrey (r.humphrey@salford.ac.uk), School of Media, Music and Performance, University of Salford, Salford M5 4WT

Sheffield Admissions Secretary (j.m.burrows@sheffield.ac.uk), Department of Music, University of Sheffield, Sheffield S10 2TN

SOAS Admissions and Recruitment (admissions@soas.ac.uk), School of Oriental and African Studies, Thornhaugh Street, Russell Square, London WC1H 0XG

Southampton Recruitment Assistant (Music) (musicbox@soton.ac.uk), Recruitment Office, School of Humanities, University of Southampton, Avenue Campus, Southampton SO17 1BJ

Southampton Solent Student Admissions (admissions@solent.ac.uk), Southampton Solent University, East Park Terrace, Southampton SO14 0RT

Staffordshire Admissions (admissions@staffs.ac.uk), Staffordshire University, College Road, Stoke on Trent ST4 2DE

Strathclyde Iain Massey (i.s.t.massey@strath.ac.uk), Department of Applied Arts, University of Strathclyde, Jordanhill Campus, Glasgow G13 1PP

Sunderland Student Recruitment (student-helpline@sunderland.ac.uk), University of Sunderland, Chester Road, Sunderland SR1 3SD

Surrey Music and sound recording (Tonmeister) Dr Slawek Zielinski (music@surrey.ac.uk); Music with computer sound design Dr Matthew Sansom (music@surrey.ac.uk); Music Dr Stephen Downes (music@surrey.ac.uk); all at Department of Music and Sound Recording, University of Surrey, Guildford GU2 7XH

Sussex Subject Co-ordinator (ug.admissions@music.sussex.ac.uk), Music, Arts B164, University of Sussex, Falmer, Brighton BN1 9RQ

Swansea IHE Gareth Jones (gareth.jones@sihe.ac.uk), Swansea Institute of Higher Education, Townhill Road, Swansea SA2 0UT

Teesside Admissions Officer (registry@tees.ac.uk), University of Teesside, Middlesbrough TS1 3BA

Thames Valley Learning Advice Centre (learning.advice@tvu.ac.uk), Thames Valley University, St Mary's Road, Ealing, London W5 5RF

Trinity C Music Admissions Co-ordinator (admissions@tcm.ac.uk), Trinity College of Music London, King Charles Court, Old Royal Naval College, Greenwich SE10 9JF

Truro C Higher Education Admissions (heinfo@trurocollege.ac.uk), Truro College, College Road, Truro, Cornwall TR1 3XX

UCE Birmingham Information Officer (enquiries@tic.ac.uk), Technology Innovation Centre, University of Central England in Birmingham, Millennium Point, Curzon Street, Birmingham B4 7XG

UCE Birmingham Conservatoire Registrar, UCE Birmingham Conservatoire, Paradise Place, Birmingham B3 3HG

Ulster Mrs H M Bracefield, Music Division, Department of Media and Performing Arts, University of Ulster, Newtownabbey BT37 0QB

Wales (UWIC) Marketing and Student Recruitment (admissions@uwic.ac.uk), University of Wales Institute, Cardiff, PO Box 377, Western Avenue, Llandaff CF5 2SG

Westminster Admissions and Marketing Office, University of Westminster, Watford Road, Northwick Park, Harrow HA1 3TP

Wolverhampton Dr Shirley Thompson (in5669@wlv.ac.uk), Music Subject Leader, University of Wolverhampton, Walsall Campus, Gorway Road, Walsall WS1 3BD

York Dr Roger Marsh, Department of Music, University of York, Heslington, York YO10 5DD

York St John Assistant Registrar (Admissions) (admissions@yorksj.ac.uk), York St John College, Lord Mayor's Walk, York YO31 7EX

Music

Part 2

Chapter 1: Introduction

Drama   Theatre is one of the most potent ways societies have invented for creating a dialogue about the values a society or culture lives by. The fact that the medium of performance/communication is the live actor serves only to heighten the immediacy of the experience. Making theatre is obviously exciting, difficult and rewarding, but to study and evaluate the contribution to human understanding of the work of theatrical practitioners can be equally rewarding, and is properly the work of universities and colleges. The study of theatre, drama or acting can be intensely absorbing, creative and instructive.

One way of studying theatre or drama is by actually doing it. In the process you may learn as much about yourself as about the subject, which can make the experience even more valuable. Many people who apply to study drama or theatre at university will have been involved in some sort of performance activity, and some may have worked professionally, and will therefore know that studying the subject at degree level is not simply a matter of working with a written text. Indeed, some courses have less to do with written drama, whether performed or studied as text, and more to do with improvisation and devising. Some courses do not allow students to be involved in extracurricular work, amateur or professional, during their course, while others positively encourage students to take whatever opportunities they can, provided it doesn't endanger their coursework; some even have periods of professional attachment.

Degree courses in drama   There is a wide variety of degree-level courses available, and they use a confusing range of terminology: 'drama', 'theatre', 'acting', 'performance' are the key terms used, though they are not always used to mean the same things, or at least not to identify the same kinds of experience a prospective student can expect. It is best to start by asking yourself what balance you would like between practical work and theoretical study of theatre/drama (see TABLE 3b in Chapter 3), and what use you intend to make of your degree. You might see yourself heading for a career in the theatre; you might be aiming to acquire a number of transferable skills; or you might hope to find both of these in one course.

If you hope to be a performer, you will benefit from a more practical course. There are differences between courses that focus on the actor and the acquisition of professional skills, devised theatre and performance, and those that examine the thing acted, for example, the play as a literary, social, educational and/or historical event. Courses aim to foster the creativity of the student, as well as to impart a body of knowledge, but they differ in the emphasis they place on these two elements. Chapter 3 will help you to identify a shortlist of courses; you should then apply to those institutions for prospectuses and course brochures, and if possible, arrange to visit those you are most interested in.

The development of modular degrees in universities has had a profound effect on drama and theatre courses. You can now combine drama with a huge range of other subjects: TABLE 2b lists what is available. Of course this means that you will work at

45

various times with very different groups of people. More specialised courses usually operate on a small group basis, which means that you will be expected to become a good team player, supporting and drawing strength from your year group.

Whatever kind of course you choose you can expect to work very hard, often at unsocial hours and weekends, and to rub shoulders with people whose very idiosyncrasy has led them to choose drama. They are likely to exasperate you and give you great joy by turns.

Dance   Dance is a relatively young subject at degree level. Most prospective students quite simply want to dance. However, you should look carefully at the different degree courses on offer, as they have different areas of strength, such as choreography, professional training or analysis. A few degree courses offer purely vocational training; the schools of dance that have traditionally supplied dancers to the various strands of the entertainment industry are still the main providers of such training, but some schools specifically focus on contemporary dance training, and not all of them give you access to loans and other help with fees. Both universities and training schools have developed courses that seek to complement the dancer's acquisition of skills with an understanding of what the various forms of dance attempt to express. For example, you might consider how dance as an art form speaks to its audience, how it expresses the ideas of the choreographer, or look at dance as an expression of society's values and ideas, or as a social, cultural or anthropological phenomenon.

The making of dance is more than just a matter of technique: as a dancer or choreographer, you must have something to say through your dance. Your study may include the forms and content of dance, the evolution of dance, improvisation and the development of styles and techniques of dance. In addition, dance has moved away from concentrating on purely European cultures. Some dance degrees place the analysis and understanding of the work of dance-makers at the centre of their course; others place the student dancer/choreographer's creativity at the core of the learning experience, encouraging the role of the performer/choreographer as the creative force behind a range of careers in dance. Some emphasise the teaching of dance or connections with the professional world through a placement. Whichever type of course you choose, you will find that working for a degree in dance is very different from attending dancing classes that simply seek to train you to execute specific steps.

Degree courses in dance   Many dance departments/institutions are small, and some are attached to or have grown out of other departments, such as physical education or performing arts. It is worth investigating how and why any dance department you are applying to has come into existence. Sometimes the ethos of a department will be influenced in some way by its relationship with other courses. Understanding something of this will enable you to make clearer and more informed choices about the course that you want to follow.

Anyone opting for a degree in dance should expect demanding workloads, sometimes with many more contact hours than other undergraduates, rigorous study and the chance of enormous creative satisfaction.

Graduate outlook   Students who have their hearts set on a performance career are not deterred by warnings of the uncertainty that surrounds employment in drama and dance, and indeed, around a fifth of those who go straight into employment after graduation do begin their careers either as performers or in work directly concerned with the stage or other media. However, some students never intend to take up a career in the field, and others change their minds or realise that they do not have the stamina or ability required. These graduates successfully enter a variety of other career areas.

Getting into drama and dance careers   Around one in five drama and dance graduates who enter employment describe themselves as working as actors, dancers or performers. Given the difficulty of gaining entry to these fields, this is quite a high proportion. Some graduates take part-time jobs unrelated to their ambitions in order to provide finance while they search for work in their chosen field, or do voluntary work to gain experience and build up contacts.

It is important to remember that a degree on its own is not a passport to a career in performance. You will be competing for jobs in acting, dance or arts administration against graduates in other subjects and, indeed, against non-graduates. While the practical work you do on your course may give you an edge, you need to gain as wide a range of experience as possible. This means spending much of your spare time building up a portfolio while at university, for example through participating in a range of different performance contexts, often without any payment. Other kinds of work experience can also broaden your horizons and develop your communication skills. Building up a network of contacts is vital to future success.

One way of improving your career chances is to take a course of professional training at a theatre or dance school. Although entry to such courses is very competitive, and finance can be difficult to obtain, such a step is well worth considering if you are determined to make a career as a performer. Others enter training a year or two after graduation, having spent time raising money to pay for the course, or gaining experience. Prospective dancers may like to visit the website of the Council for Dance Education and Training at www.cdet.org.uk for information on dance training and opportunities. Similar information is available for drama students on the National Council for Drama Training's website at www.ncdt.co.uk.

Teaching is an obvious option for those who wish to use their subject in their career (those who wish to teach in a state school need to take the one-year postgraduate certificate in education, or PGCE). For further information about teaching careers, visit the Training and Development Agency for Schools website at www.tda.gov.uk.

Other drama- and dance-related opportunities   A number of drama and dance graduates are interested in developing careers in dance and movement therapy and drama therapy. A professional training course is necessary, and these are often available on a part-time basis, but require experience and maturity. First steps into these careers on graduation may therefore involve gaining a range of experience, possibly on a voluntary basis. You should also use your time at university to make contact with practitioners and gain valuable experience. For further information, see the website of the Association of Dance Movement Therapy at www.admt.org.uk.

Arts administration is another area of interest to those on performance courses, but competition is fierce for the few vacancies that arise. Gaining experience, for instance with college-based events, local festivals or arts centres, and making contacts while at university or college are vital. Experience gained outside the arts field in areas such as marketing, administration or sales may also stand you in good stead. To find out more about this field see the Arts Marketing Association's website at www.a-m-a.co.uk.

TABLE 2a lists the specialised and combined courses at universities and colleges in the UK that lead to the award of an honours degree in drama or dance. You should refer to the notes preceding TABLE 2a in the first part of this Guide for guidance on using the table.

Table 2a	First-degree courses in **Drama and Dance**								
Institution Course title	① ② ③ see combined subject list – Table 2b	**Degree**	**Duration** Number of years	**Foundation year** ● at this institution ○ of franchised institution ◑ second-year entry	**Modes of study** ● full time; ➤ part time ○ time abroad ◑ sandwich	**Modular scheme** ✿	**Course type** ● specialised; ◑ combined	**No of combined courses**
ALRA www.alra.co.uk								
Acting		BA	3		●		●	0
Aberystwyth www.aber.ac.uk								
Drama ①		BA	3		● ➤		● ◑	19
Performance studies ②		BA	3		● ➤		● ◑	8
Anglia Ruskin www.anglia.ac.uk								
Drama		BA	3		●		● ◑	5
Arts Institute at Bournemouth www.aib.ac.uk								
Acting for theatre, film and television		BA	3		●		●	0
Bangor www.bangor.ac.uk								
Theatre studies		BA	3		● ➤	✿	● ◑	2
Bath Spa www.bathspa.ac.uk								
Dance ①		BA	3		● ➤	✿	● ◑	17
Drama studies ②		BA	3		●	✿	● ◑	20
Performing arts		BA	3	○	●		●	0
Belfast www.qub.ac.uk								
Drama		BA	3		●		● ◑	11
Birmingham www.bham.ac.uk								
Drama and theatre arts		BA	3		●		● ◑	10
Bishop Grosseteste C www.bgc.ac.uk								
Drama in the community		BA	3		● ➤		●	0
Brighton www.brighton.ac.uk								
Dance and visual art ①		BA	3		● ➤		◑	1
Theatre and visual art ②		BA	3		● ➤		◑	1
Bristol www.bris.ac.uk								
Drama		BA	3		●		● ◑	6
Bristol UWE www.uwe.ac.uk								
Drama		BA	3		● ➤	✿	● ◑	21
Brunel www.brunel.ac.uk								
Modern drama studies		BA	3		● ➤	✿	● ◑	3
Buckinghamshire Chilterns UC www.bcuc.ac.uk								
Drama		BA	3		●	✿	◑	7
Central Lancashire www.uclan.ac.uk								
Acting		BA	3		●		●	0
English and theatre studies ①		BA	3		● ➤		◑	1
Music theatre		BA	3		● ➤		●	0
Theatre practice		BA	3	○	● ➤		●	0

First-degree courses in **Drama and Dance**

Institution / Course title	①②③ see combined subject list – Table 2b	Degree	Duration (years)	Foundation year: at this institution	Foundation year: at franchised institution	Foundation year: second-year entry	Modes of study: full time	Modes of study: part time	Modes of study: time abroad	Modes of study: sandwich	Modular scheme	Course type (specialised ●; combined ◐)	No of combined courses
Central S Speech & Drama www.cssd.ac.uk													
Acting		BA	3				●					●	0
Drama, applied theatre and education ①		BA	3				●					◐	1
Chester www.chester.ac.uk													
Dance ①		BA	3				●				●	● ◐	27
Drama and theatre studies ②		BA	3				●				●	● ◐	30
Chichester www.chiuni.ac.uk													
Dance ①		BA	3				●	⌣			●	● ◐	14
Performing arts ②		BA	3				●	⌣			●	● ◐	13
City C Manchester www.ccm.ac.uk													
Acting studies		BA	4				●					●	0
Musical theatre studies		BA	3				●					●	0
Colchester I www.colch-inst.ac.uk													
Musical theatre		BA	3				●					●	0
Coventry www.coventry.ac.uk													
Dance and professional practice		BA	3				●	⌣				●	0
Dance, theatre and professional practice		BA	3				●	⌣				●	0
Theatre and professional practice		BA	3				●	⌣				●	0
Cumbria I www.cumbria.ac.uk													
Dance ①		BA	3				●					◐	3
Drama ②		BA	3				●					◐	4
Music theatre ③		BA	3				●					◐	5
Performing arts		BA	3				●	⌣				●	0
Dartington CA www.dartington.ac.uk													
Choreography ①		BA	3				●					● ◐	5
Theatre ②		BA	3				●					● ◐	5
De Montfort www.dmu.ac.uk													
Dance ①		BA	3				●	⌣				● ◐	4
Drama studies ②		BA	3				●	⌣				● ◐	6
Performing arts		BA	3	●			●	⌣				●	0
Derby www.derby.ac.uk													
Dance and movement studies ①		BA	3				●					◐	6
Theatre arts		BA	3				●					●	0
Theatre studies ②		BA	3				●	⌣			●	◐	17
Doncaster C www.don.ac.uk													
Dance practice with digital performance		BA	3				●					●	0
Theatre practice with digital performance		BA	3				●					●	0
East Anglia www.uea.ac.uk													
Drama		BA	3				●				●	● ◐	1
East London www.uel.ac.uk													
Dance		BA	3				●					●	0
Performing arts ①		BA	3	●	○		●		○			● ◐	5
Theatre studies		BA	3				●					●	0
Edge Hill www.edgehill.ac.uk													
Dance		BA	3				●	⌣				●	0
Drama ①		BA	3				●	⌣			●	● ◐	7
Drama, physical theatre and dance		BA	3				●	⌣				●	0
Essex www.essex.ac.uk													
Drama		BA	3				●					● ◐	2

First-degree courses in **Drama and Dance**

Institution / Course title	①②③ see combined subject list – Table 2b	Degree	Duration (Number of years)	Foundation year	Modes of study	Modular scheme	Course type	No of combined courses
Exeter www.exeter.ac.uk								
Drama		BA	3		●		●	0
Glamorgan www.glam.ac.uk								
Drama (theatre and media)		BA	3		● ⌐	⊕	● ◑	6
Glasgow www.gla.ac.uk								
Theatre studies		MA	4	◐	●	⊕	● ◑	32
Goldsmiths www.goldsmiths.ac.uk								
Drama and theatre arts		BA	3		●		●	0
English and drama ①		BA	3		●		◑	1
Greenwich www.gre.ac.uk								
Dance and theatre performance		BA	3		●		●	0
Drama ①		BA	3		●		● ◑	4
Guildhall S Music & Drama www.gsmd.ac.uk								
Acting		BA	3		●		●	0
Huddersfield www.hud.ac.uk								
Drama		BA	3		● ⌐	⊕	● ◑	3
Hull www.hull.ac.uk								
Drama ①		BA	3		●	⊕	● ◑	10
Theatre and performance studies ②		BA	3		● ⌐		● ◑	3
Kent www.ukc.ac.uk								
Drama and theatre studies		BA	4		●		● ◑	11
Kingston www.kingston.ac.uk								
Drama		BA	3		● ⌐ ○		● ◑	13
Laban www.laban.org								
Dance theatre		BA	3		●		●	0
Lancaster www.lancs.ac.uk								
Theatre studies		BA	3		●		● ◑	3
Leeds www.leeds.ac.uk								
Dance		BA	3		● ⌐		●	0
English literature and theatre studies ①		BA	3, 4		● ○		◑	1
Theatre and performance		BA	3		● ◑		●	0
Lincoln www.lincoln.ac.uk								
Drama		BA	3		●		● ◑	4
Liverpool Hope www.hope.ac.uk								
Creative and performing arts		BA	3		● ⌐		●	0
Dance ①		BA	3		● ⌐		◑	24
Drama and theatre studies ②		BA	3		● ⌐	⊕	● ◑	26
LIPA www.lipa.ac.uk								
Acting (performing arts)		BA	3		●		●	0
Dance (performing arts)		BA	3		●		●	0
Liverpool John Moores www.ljmu.ac.uk								
Dance studies		BA	3		●		●	0
Drama ①		BA	3		●		● ◑	4
London Metropolitan www.londonmet.ac.uk								
Performing arts		BA	3		●		●	0
Theatre studies ①		BA	3		●	⊕	● ◑	7
London South Bank www.sbu.ac.uk								
Acting		BA	3		●		●	0
Drama and performance studies		BA	3		●		●	0

(continued) Table 2a

First-degree courses in **Drama and Dance**

Institution / Course title	①②③ see combined subject list – Table 2b	Degree	Duration (Number of years)	Foundation year (● at this institution / ○ at franchised institution / ◑ second-year entry)	Modes of study (● full time; ⌣ part time / time abroad / sandwich)	Modular scheme	Course type (● specialised; ◑ combined)	No of combined courses
Loughborough www.lboro.ac.uk								
Drama		BA	3		●		● ◑	1
Manchester www.man.ac.uk								
Drama		BA	3		●		● ◑	3
Manchester Metropolitan www.mmu.ac.uk								
Acting		BA	3		●		●	0
Contemporary theatre and performance		BA	3		●		●	0
Dance ①		BA	3		● ⌣	✿	● ◑	24
Drama ②		BA	3		● ⌣	✿	◑	24
Marjon www.marjon.ac.uk								
Drama		BA	3		●	✿	● ◑	10
Middlesex www.mdx.ac.uk								
Dance performance		BA	3		●		●	0
Dance studies		BA	3		●		●	0
Dance with performing arts		BA	3		●		●	0
Drama and theatre arts ①		BA	3		●	✿	● ◑	10
Mountview ATA www.mountview.ac.uk								
Acting		BA	3		●		●	0
Musical theatre		BA	3		●		●	0
Newman C www.newman.ac.uk								
Drama		BA	3		●	✿	● ◑	8
North East Wales I www.newi.ac.uk								
Theatre and performance		BA	3		●		● ◑	1
Northampton www.northampton.ac.uk								
Dance ①		BA	3		● ⌣	✿	● ◑	22
Drama ②		BA/BSc	3		● ⌣	✿	● ◑	27
Performance ③		BA	3		●	✿	● ◑	19
Northumbria www.northumbria.ac.uk								
Dance/choreography		BA	3		●		●	0
Drama		BA	3		●		●	0
Performance		BA	3		●		●	0
Oxford Brookes www.brookes.ac.uk								
Performing arts		BA	3		●	✿	◑	47
Peterborough RC www.peterborough.ac.uk								
Performing arts		BA	3		●		●	0
Plymouth www.plymouth.ac.uk								
Theatre and performance		BA	3		● ⌣		●	0
Portsmouth www.port.ac.uk								
Drama		BA	3		●		◑	4
Queen Margaret www.qmu.ac.uk								
Acting and performance		BA	4	◑	●		●	0
Drama and theatre arts		BA	4	◑	● ⌣		●	0
Queen Mary www.qmul.ac.uk								
Drama		BA	3		●		● ◑	6
Reading www.rdg.ac.uk								
Film and theatre		BA	3		●		● ◑	5
Roehampton www.roehampton.ac.uk								
Dance studies ①		BA/BSc	3	●	● ⌣ ○	✿	● ◑	27
Drama and theatre studies ②		BA/BSc	3	●	● ⌣ ○	✿	● ◑	27

First-degree courses in **Drama and Dance**

Institution / Course title	① ② ③ see combined subject list – Table 2b	Degree	Duration (Number of years)	Foundation year	Modes of study	Modular scheme	Course type	No of combined courses
Rose Bruford C www.bruford.ac.uk								
Acting		BA	3		●		●	0
Actor-musician ①		BA	3		●		◑	1
Directing		BA	3		●		●	0
European/American theatre arts		BA	3		●		●	0
Royal Academy of Dance www.rad.org.uk								
Ballet education		BA	3		●		●	0
Royal Holloway www.rhul.ac.uk								
Drama and theatre studies ①		BA	3	●	●		● ◑	7
International theatre (Australia/France)		BA	4		○		●	0
Royal Scottish A Music & Drama www.rsamd.ac.uk								
Contemporary theatre practice		BA	4		●		●	0
Royal Welsh C Music & Drama www.rwcmd.ac.uk								
Acting		BA	3		●		●	0
St Martin's C www.ucsm.ac.uk								
Drama		BA	3		● ◕	✿	● ◑	3
St Mary's C www.smuc.ac.uk								
Drama and performance studies ①		BA	3		● ◕		● ◑	7
Physical theatre ②		BA	3		● ◕		● ◑	5
Salford www.salford.ac.uk								
Contemporary theatre practice		BA	3		●		●	0
Performing arts ①		BA	3, 4		●		◑	1
Sheffield www.sheffield.ac.uk								
English and drama		BA	3		●		◑	1
Southampton Solent www.solent.ac.uk								
Performance		BA	3		●		●	0
Staffordshire www.staffs.ac.uk								
Theatre arts ①		BA	3		● ◕		◑	5
Theatre studies ②		BA	3		● ◕		◑	7
Sunderland www.sunderland.ac.uk								
Dance ①		BA	3		●		◑	25
Performing arts studies		BA	3		●		●	0
Surrey www.surrey.ac.uk								
Dance and culture		BA	3, 4		● ◑		●	0
Sussex www.sussex.ac.uk								
Drama studies		BA	3		●		◑	5
Swansea IHE www.sihe.ac.uk								
Performing arts and theatre studies		BA	3		● ◕		◑	0
Thames Valley www.tvu.ac.uk								
Drama: acting for stage and media		BA	3		●		●	0
Theatre		BA	3		●		●	0
Trinity C (Carmarthen) www.trinity-cm.ac.uk								
Acting		BA	3		●		●	0
Theatre studies		BA	3		●		●	0
UC Suffolk www.ucs.ac.uk								
Performing arts		BA	3		●		●	0
UCE Birmingham www.uce.ac.uk								
English and drama		BA	3		● ◕		◑	1

Drama and Dance

53

(continued) Table 2a

First-degree courses in **Drama and Dance**

Institution / Course title	①②③ see combined subject list – Table 2b	Degree	Duration (No. of years)	Foundation year	Modes of study	Modular scheme	Course type	No of combined courses
Ulster www.ulster.ac.uk								
Dance ①		BA	3		●		● ◑	7
Drama ②		BA	3		● ○	🌀	● ◑	9
University of the Arts London www.arts.ac.uk								
Acting		BA	3		●		●	0
Directing		BA	3		●		●	0
Wales (UWIC) www.uwic.ac.uk								
Dance		BA	3		● ➤		●	0
Warwick www.warwick.ac.uk								
Theatre and performance studies		BA	3		●		● ◑	1
Winchester www.winchester.ac.uk								
Choreography and dance studies ①		BA	3		● ➤	🌀	● ◑	16
Drama ②		BA	3		● ➤	🌀	● ◑	18
Drama, community theatre and media		BA	3		●		●	0
Performing arts ③		BA	3		●	🌀	● ◑	17
Wolverhampton www.wlv.ac.uk								
Dance practice and performance ①		BA	3		● ➤	🌀	● ◑	9
Drama and performance ②		BA	3		● ➤	🌀	● ◑	14
Worcester www.worcester.ac.uk								
Drama and performance studies		BA	3	○	● ➤	🌀	● ◑	14
York St John www.yorksj.ac.uk								
Performance: dance		BA	3		● ➤	🌀	●	0
Performance: theatre		BA	3		● ➤	🌀	●	0
Theatre ①		BA	3		● ➤		◑	4

Subjects available in combination with drama and dance

TABLE 2b shows subjects that can make up one-third to half of your degree programme when combined with drama or dance in the degrees listed in TABLE 2a. Where there is a number after the institution, this identifies which of the courses in TABLE 2a offer that subject.

Table 2b

Subjects to combine with **Drama or Dance**

Accountancy/accounting Bristol UWE, Northampton②③, Oxford Brookes
African/Caribbean studies London Metropolitan①
American literature Winchester②③
American studies Aberystwyth①, Derby②, Hull①, Lincoln, Manchester Metropolitan①②, Northampton①②③, Sunderland①, Winchester②③, Worcester
Animal biology Worcester
Anthropology Glasgow, Oxford Brookes, Roehampton①②
Applied social science Manchester Metropolitan①②
Archaeology Chester①②, Winchester③

Art Bath Spa①②, Reading
Art and design Newman C, Worcester
Art history Aberystwyth①, Birmingham, Glasgow, Hull①, Kingston, Northampton①②, Oxford Brookes, Reading, Roehampton①②, Sunderland①
Artificial intelligence Oxford Brookes
Arts management De Montfort①②, London Metropolitan①, Manchester Metropolitan①②, Oxford Brookes
Biology Bath Spa①②, Oxford Brookes, Roehampton①②
Business information systems East London①
Business mathematics Bristol UWE

Subjects to combine with **Drama or Dance**

Business studies Bath Spa① ②, Bristol UWE, Chester① ②, Chichester① ②, Derby②, Liverpool Hope②, Manchester Metropolitan① ②, Middlesex①, Northampton① ②, Oxford Brookes, Roehampton① ②, Sunderland①, Winchester① ② ③, Worcester

Chemistry Sunderland①

Childhood studies Bristol UWE, Liverpool Hope① ②, Manchester Metropolitan① ②, Oxford Brookes, Roehampton① ②, Winchester②

Classical archaeology Kent

Classical studies Birmingham, Roehampton① ②, Royal Holloway①

Communication studies Bath Spa① ②, Chester① ②, Oxford Brookes, Worcester, York St John①

Community studies East London①

Comparative literature Glasgow, Kent

Computer science Chester① ②

Computing Bristol UWE, Glasgow, Liverpool Hope①, Oxford Brookes, Sunderland①, Worcester

Counselling Chester②, Newman C

Creative writing Anglia Ruskin, Bath Spa① ②, Buckinghamshire Chilterns UC, Chester① ②, Chichester① ②, Cumbria I① ② ③, De Montfort②, Derby②, Edge Hill①, Kingston, Liverpool John Moores①, Manchester Metropolitan① ②, Marjon, Middlesex①, Northampton① ② ③, Portsmouth, Roehampton① ②, Royal Holloway①, St Martin's C, St Mary's C① ②, Staffordshire②, Winchester① ② ③, Wolverhampton②

Criminology Bristol UWE, Chester②, Edge Hill①, Manchester Metropolitan① ②, Northampton②, Roehampton②, Staffordshire②, Sunderland①

Cultural studies Bath Spa②, Cumbria I① ② ③, Derby②, Manchester Metropolitan① ②, Sussex

Czech Glasgow

Dance Bath Spa②, Chester②, Chichester②, Cumbria I① ② ③, Dartington CA②, De Montfort②, Derby②, Hull①, Liverpool Hope②, Manchester Metropolitan②, Northampton② ③, Roehampton②, Ulster②, Winchester②, Wolverhampton②

Deaf studies Wolverhampton①

Development studies Chester① ②

Drama Aberystwyth②, Bath Spa①, Chester①, Cumbria I① ②, De Montfort①, Liverpool Hope①, Manchester Metropolitan①, Northampton① ②, Roehampton①, St Mary's C①, Staffordshire①, Ulster①, Winchester① ② ③, Wolverhampton①

East European studies Glasgow

East Mediterranean history Birmingham

Ecology Oxford Brookes

Economic/social history Glasgow

Economics Glasgow, Northampton①, Oxford Brookes

Education Aberystwyth① ②, Bath Spa① ②, Bristol UWE, Chester②, De Montfort②, Derby②, Edge Hill①, Greenwich①, Liverpool Hope① ②, Manchester Metropolitan① ②, Marjon, Newman C, Northampton① ②, Oxford Brookes, Roehampton① ②, St Martin's C, Sunderland①, Winchester① ②, Wolverhampton① ②

English Anglia Ruskin, Belfast, Birmingham, Bristol, Bristol UWE, Brunel, Central Lancashire①, Chester① ②, Chichester① ②, De Montfort①, Derby① ②, Edge Hill①, Glamorgan, Goldsmiths①, Huddersfield, Hull① ②, Lincoln, Liverpool John Moores①, Loughborough, Manchester, Manchester Metropolitan① ②, Newman C, Northampton②, Oxford Brookes, Portsmouth, Queen Mary, Reading, Royal Holloway①, St Martin's C, St Mary's C① ②, Sheffield, Sunderland①, Sussex, UCE Birmingham, Warwick, Winchester① ② ③, Wolverhampton②, Worcester

English as a foreign language Chichester① ②

English language Bristol UWE, Glasgow, Kingston, Liverpool Hope① ②, London Metropolitan①, Oxford Brookes, Roehampton① ②

English literature Aberystwyth① ②, Bath Spa① ②, Buckinghamshire Chilterns UC, East Anglia, Glasgow, Kent, Kingston, Lancaster, Leeds①, Liverpool Hope②, London Metropolitan①, Marjon, Middlesex①, Roehampton① ②, York St John①

Enterprise/entrepreneurship Chichester① ②, Dartington CA① ②, Northampton② ③

Environmental management Liverpool Hope①

Environmental science Bristol UWE, Oxford Brookes

Equine studies Northampton① ② ③

European studies Sunderland①

Exercise science Oxford Brookes

Film/television studies Aberystwyth① ②, Anglia Ruskin, Bath Spa① ②, Belfast, Bristol UWE, Brunel, Buckinghamshire Chilterns UC, Derby① ②, Glamorgan, Glasgow, Hull①, Kent, Kingston, Liverpool Hope① ②, Liverpool John Moores①, London Metropolitan①, Manchester, Manchester Metropolitan①, Oxford Brookes, Portsmouth, Queen Mary, Roehampton①, St Mary's C①, Staffordshire①, Sussex, Winchester①, Wolverhampton②, Worcester, York St John①

Fine art Aberystwyth①, Chester① ②, Chichester① ②, Liverpool Hope① ②, Northampton②, York St John①

Food studies Bath Spa① ②

Forensic science Liverpool Hope②

French Aberystwyth①, Belfast, Bristol, Chester① ②, Glasgow, Hull①, Kent, Kingston, Middlesex①, Northampton② ③, Queen Mary, Roehampton① ②, Royal Holloway①, Ulster① ②

55

Table 2b (continued)

Subjects to combine with **Drama or Dance**

French studies   Birmingham, Lancaster, Oxford Brookes
Gender studies   Sunderland ①, Sussex
Geographical information systems   Bath Spa ②
Geography   Bath Spa ① ②, Bristol UWE, Chester ① ②, Glasgow, Liverpool Hope ① ②, Marjon, Oxford Brookes, Sunderland ①
German   Aberystwyth ①, Bristol, Chester ① ②, Glasgow, Hull ①, Kent, Middlesex ①, Northampton ① ② ③, Queen Mary, Reading, Royal Holloway ①, Ulster ① ②
German studies   Birmingham
Greek   Glasgow
Health studies   Bath Spa ① ②, Liverpool Hope ①, Manchester Metropolitan ① ②, Northampton ① ③, Roehampton ①, St Mary's C ②, Sunderland ①, Wolverhampton ①
Hispanic studies   Glasgow, Kent, Queen Mary
History   Aberystwyth ①, Bath Spa ① ②, Bristol UWE, Chester ① ②, Derby ②, Glamorgan, Glasgow, Greenwich ①, Kent, Kingston, Lincoln, Liverpool Hope ①, London Metropolitan ①, Marjon, Northampton ① ③, Oxford Brookes, Roehampton ① ②, Sunderland ①, Winchester ① ② ③, Wolverhampton ②, Worcester
Hospitality management   Oxford Brookes
Human biology   Liverpool Hope ②, Oxford Brookes, Roehampton ① ②
Human geography   Aberystwyth ①, Northampton ②
Human resource management   Derby ①, East London ①, Manchester Metropolitan ① ②, Northampton ②
Information systems   Bristol UWE, Derby ②, Oxford Brookes
Information technology   Chichester ①, Edge Hill ①, Liverpool Hope ① ②, Manchester Metropolitan ① ②, Northampton ① ②
International politics   Aberystwyth ① ②, Ulster ②, Winchester ① ② ③
International studies/relations   Oxford Brookes
Internet technology   Chester ① ②, Liverpool Hope ① ②
Irish   Aberystwyth ①, Ulster ① ②
Irish studies   Liverpool Hope ① ②, St Mary's C ①
Italian   Bristol, Glasgow, Hull ①, Kent, Middlesex ①, Reading, Royal Holloway ①
Italian studies   Birmingham
Japanese studies   Oxford Brookes
Journalism   Buckinghamshire Chilterns UC, Chester ① ②, Middlesex ①, Roehampton ① ②, Staffordshire ① ②, Sunderland ①, Winchester ① ② ③
Law   Derby ②, Liverpool Hope ① ②, Northampton ① ②, Oxford Brookes

Legal studies   Manchester Metropolitan ① ②
Leisure management   Oxford Brookes, Winchester ① ② ③, Wolverhampton ①
Leisure studies   Liverpool Hope ②, Manchester Metropolitan ① ②
Library and information studies   Aberystwyth ①
Linguistics   Belfast, Sunderland ①
Literature   Essex
Management studies   Edge Hill ①, Marjon, Newman C, Northampton ②
Marketing   Bristol UWE, Chester ① ②, Chichester ②, Derby ① ②, East London ①, Liverpool Hope ②, Manchester Metropolitan ① ②, Northampton ① ②, Oxford Brookes, Ulster ②
Mathematics   Aberystwyth ①, Chester ① ②, Derby ②, Glasgow, Northampton ②, Oxford Brookes
Media studies   Anglia Ruskin, Bangor, Birmingham, Bristol UWE, Buckinghamshire Chilterns UC, Chichester ① ②, De Montfort ②, Edge Hill ①, Glamorgan, Huddersfield, Kingston, Lincoln, Liverpool Hope ②, Liverpool John Moores ①, Marjon, Newman C, North East Wales I, Northampton ① ②, Portsmouth, St Mary's C ① ②, Salford ①, Staffordshire ① ②, Sunderland ①, Winchester ①, Wolverhampton ②, Worcester
Modern history   Belfast, Staffordshire ②
Modern languages   Essex, Sussex
Molecular biology   Oxford Brookes
Multimedia   Chester ① ②, Oxford Brookes
Music   Bath Spa ① ②, Birmingham, Brunel, Chichester ① ②, Glasgow, Huddersfield, Hull ①, Liverpool Hope ① ②, Manchester, Manchester Metropolitan ① ②, Oxford Brookes, Roehampton ① ②, Rose Bruford C ①, Royal Holloway ①, Sunderland ①, Ulster ① ②, Wolverhampton ① ②
Music technology   Bristol UWE, Chichester ① ②, Liverpool Hope ②
Nutrition   Liverpool Hope ②, Oxford Brookes
Performance studies   Aberystwyth ①, Chester ①, Chichester ①, Dartington CA ① ②, De Montfort ①, Middlesex ①, Northampton ① ②, Winchester ① ②
Philosophy   Anglia Ruskin, Bristol UWE, Glasgow, Greenwich ①, Kent, Manchester Metropolitan ① ②, Newman C, Northampton ① ③, Oxford Brookes, Roehampton ① ②, St Mary's C ①, Staffordshire ① ②, Wolverhampton ②
Photography   De Montfort ①, Roehampton ① ②, Sunderland ①
Physical geography   Northampton ① ②, Oxford Brookes
Physics   Glasgow
Physiology   Sunderland ①
Polish   Glasgow
Politics   Aberystwyth ① ②, Belfast, Bristol UWE, Glasgow, Greenwich ①, Kingston, Liverpool

Subjects to combine with **Drama or Dance**

Hope②, Northampton① ②, Oxford Brookes, Sunderland①
Portuguese　Birmingham, Bristol
Psychology　Bath Spa① ②, Bristol UWE, Chester②, Derby②, Glasgow, Kingston, Liverpool Hope① ②, Manchester Metropolitan① ②, Northampton① ② ③, Oxford Brookes, Roehampton① ② ③, Sunderland①, Ulster① ②, Winchester① ② ③, Wolverhampton①, Worcester
Public policy　Glasgow
Public relations　Marjon, Sunderland①
Publishing　Middlesex①, Oxford Brookes
Religious studies　Bath Spa① ②, Kent, Oxford Brookes, Roehampton① ②
Retailing　Oxford Brookes
Russian　Glasgow, Queen Mary
Scholastic philosophy　Belfast
Scottish history　Glasgow
Scottish literature　Glasgow
Social anthropology　Belfast, Roehampton①
Social psychology　Newman C
Sociology　Bath Spa②, Belfast, Bristol UWE, Chester① ②, Derby②, Glasgow, Kingston, Liverpool Hope①, Manchester Metropolitan① ②, Marjon, Northampton① ②, Oxford Brookes, Roehampton① ②, Staffordshire②, Sunderland①, Wolverhampton②, Worcester
Software engineering　Oxford Brookes

Spanish　Aberystwyth①, Belfast, Bristol, Chester① ②, Hull①, Kingston, Middlesex①, Roehampton① ②, Ulster① ②
Spanish studies　Lancaster
Sports science　Chester① ②, Roehampton①, Wolverhampton①
Sports studies　Derby②, Liverpool Hope① ②, Manchester Metropolitan① ②, Marjon, Northampton① ②, Oxford Brookes, Roehampton① ②, Winchester① ②, Wolverhampton①
Statistics　Oxford Brookes
TEFL　Sunderland①
Textile design　Bath Spa① ②
Theatre studies　Cumbria I① ② ②, Dartington CA①, Derby①
Theology　Belfast, Chester① ②, Glasgow, Hull①, Liverpool Hope① ②, Oxford Brookes, Roehampton① ②, St Mary's C①, Winchester② ②
Third world studies　Northampton① ②
Tourism　Chester① ②, Liverpool Hope① ②, Northampton②, Oxford Brookes, Sunderland①, Winchester② ②, Wolverhampton①
Urban studies　Chester① ②
Visual art　Brighton① ②, Dartington CA① ②, Worcester
Visual studies　Buckinghamshire Chilterns UC
War studies　Liverpool Hope① ②
Welsh　Aberystwyth① ②, Bangor
Welsh history　Aberystwyth①

Other courses that may interest you　If you are interested in drama or dance, the following courses may also interest you:

- Literary studies and drama (Manchester)
- Dance available as a minor subject only (Hull)
- Acting (ordinary degree) (Royal Scottish A Music & Drama)
- Stage management and theatre production (Central S Speech & Drama, London South Bank, Queen Margaret, Rose Bruford C and Royal Welsh C Music & Drama)
- Stage design and management studies (City C Manchester)
- Technical theatre arts (Middlesex)
- Scenic arts (Rose Bruford C)
- Scriptwriting and performance (East Anglia)
- Children's theatre (Edge Hill)
- Puppetry (Central S Speech & Drama)
- Costume and make-up for the performing arts (University of the Arts London).

You may also like to look at other Degree Course Guides, such as those for *English, Media Studies and American Studies*, or *Art and Design Studies* (which includes theatre design).

Drama and Dance

Course content   TABLE 3a shows the topics or activities that are offered on each course. The following paragraphs introduce or explain some of the terms used in the table.

Performance   This term is used in a variety of contexts and may be used to mean full-scale productions or as a more general term to encompass a range of performance styles/genres. Courses that put some emphasis upon performance often use it as a way of assessing the student's acquisition of skills.

Directing   This is often an option, rather than compulsory. It can be a chance to take on total responsibility for the creative realisation of a production.

Production   Most courses use this word to denote all the activities that are undertaken during the process of preparing a piece for performance. It can mean that you get to try your hand at all aspects of backstage and technical work, from lighting to digital editing. However, many courses allow the student to specialise in some chosen aspect of production at an early stage.

Stage design   Specialist courses in scenography have grown out of schools of art. When this type of work is offered as part of a drama degree, the important factors are to do with specialist training and the possibility of designs being realised in production.

History of theatre or dance   This need not be purely book- or video-based. Some courses approach such learning experientially, attempting to recreate for the student the circumstances of historical performance.

Analysis   This may be done through live performance, videos of performance or text. Sometimes it means the practical performance of scenes from set plays, improvisations or repertory from choreographic works, or it can be the mechanism for the comparative analysis of different stylistic or historical solutions to the communication of a playwright's or choreographer's ideas.

Radio/television/video/film   This may cover both technical and performance aspects of the particular medium. It may be focused on the analysis of examples of the medium as reflections of the culture they were made for, or as examples of the aesthetic of the medium.

New media   This term may be used in a variety of performance contexts and is a general term relating to the use of video/DVD, digital imaging, interactive media, light and sound.

Community   Performance within the community may involve the professional creation of work for a variety of different client groups within the community, for example: youth groups, older people, people with disabilities, prisoners, children and so on. Beyond the creative context itself, study may include practical projects, methods of teaching, organising and funding and the general study of the use of performance in these contexts. The notion and origin of the term 'community' may also be examined.

Education   This covers the application of dance within an educational context. Areas that might be considered include the historical development of performance in schools, its place within the National Curriculum, methods of teaching and planning, and opportunities for teaching practice within an educational context.

Mime/ballet   These are highly specialised areas of study, usually focused on the individual acquisition of skills.

Contemporary dance   This should refer to dance within a contemporary context, but the term is often used rather loosely. Find out exactly what is meant by it in the courses you are interested in.

Choreography   This refers to making dances. Some courses are particularly distinctive in the emphasis they place on choreography and the performer/maker. The particular balance of practical work in this area differs from course to course, and is an important consideration for many students. Find out exactly how much time is given to making your own work.

Table 3a — Course content

Institution / Course title · ○ optional; ● compulsory; ◐ compulsory + options · ①②: see notes after table

Institution / Course title	Performance	Directing	Production	Stage design	Stage/studio management	History of theatre or dance	Textual analysis	Scriptwriting	Radio	Television	Film	Video	Wardrobe/make-up	Drama/dance in the community	Drama/dance in education	Administration	Mime	Ballet	Contemporary dance	Jazz dance	Non-Western/other dance styles	Choreography	Dance notation	Dance analysis
Aberystwyth																								
Drama ①	○	○	○	○	○	○	●	○	○	○	○	○	○	○	○	○	○							
Performance studies ②	●	○													○	○					○			
Anglia Ruskin																								
Drama ①	○	○	○	○	○	●	●	○	○	○	○	○												
Arts Institute at Bournemouth																								
Acting for theatre, film and television	●		●			●					●	●												
Bangor																								
Theatre studies	●	○	○	◐	○	○	◐	○	○	○	○		●	○										
Bath Spa																								
Dance ①	●		○	○		●	◐					●	●	○	●	●	○		●			○	●	●
Drama studies	●	●				●	●			○						○								
Performing arts	○	○	○	○	○	○	○	○	○	○	○	○				○								
Birmingham																								
Drama and theatre arts	◐	○	●	○	●	◐	●	○	○			○	○	●		○	○		○					

Drama and Dance

Course content

Key: ○ optional; ● compulsory; ◑ compulsory + options; ① ② : see notes after table

Institution / Course title	Performance	Directing	Production	Stage design	Stage/studio management	History of theatre or dance	Textual analysis	Scriptwriting	Radio	Television	Film	Video	Wardrobe/makeup	Drama/dance in the community	Drama/dance in education	Administration	Mime	Ballet	Contemporary dance	Jazz dance	Non-Western/other dance styles	Choreography	Dance notation	Dance analysis
Bishop Grosseteste C																								
Drama in the community	●	●	●	○	◑	●	●	◑	◑				◑	●	●	●	◑		●		○	○		○
Brighton																								
Dance and visual art ①	●					●	●				●								●			●	●	●
Theatre and visual art ②		○	○	○	○		○	○		○	○		○									○		
Bristol																								
Drama ①	○	○	○	○	○	◑	◑	○		◑	◑	○	○	○	○	○								
Bristol UWE																								
Drama ①	○	○				○	○			○														
Brunel																								
Modern drama studies ①	●	○	○			●	○	○						○	○	○			○					
Buckinghamshire Chilterns UC																								
Drama	●	●	●	●	○	◑	●	●		○	○	○					●							
Central Lancashire																								
Acting ①	●	●	●	○	◑	●	●		●	●			○	○	○									
English and theatre studies ②	○	○				●	●	○		○														
Music theatre ③	●	◑	●	○	○		●	◑																
Theatre practice	●	●	●	◑	◑		●	◑					○			○			○		○	○		○
Chester																								
Dance	●	○	○	●	○	●	○	○	○	○	○	○	○	●	●	○	○	●	●			●	○	●
Drama and theatre studies	●	○	○	●	●	●	○	○	○	○	○	○	○	●	●	○	○	●	●			○	○	○
Chichester																								
Dance ①	●		○		○	●	◑	○	○				○	○	◑		○	●	◑		◑	●	○	◑
Performing arts	●		●	○	●				○	○	○		○	○	○									
City C Manchester																								
Acting studies	●	○				●	●	○		●									●	○		●		
Coventry																								
Dance and professional practice ①	●													○	○	●			●	●		●		●
Theatre and professional practice ②	●	○	●			●	●							○		●								
Cumbria I																								
Dance																			○	○	○	○	○	○
Performing arts	●		●	○	●		◑		◑	◑		○			●									
De Montfort																								
Dance ①	●										●			○	○				●					
Drama studies	○	○												○										
Performing arts ②	●	●	●		●		●							●		●			●			●		●
Derby																								
Theatre studies	◑	◑	◑	○	○	◑	◑	○	○	○	○			○	○				◑			◑	○	
East Anglia																								
Drama	◑	○	○	○	○	◑	◑	○		○	○	○			○									
East London																								
Performing arts ①	●	●		●			●							●	●									
Edge Hill																								
Drama	●	●	●	○	●	●	●	◑		●		●		○		○								
Drama, physical theatre and dance ①	●		●		●	●	●		○				○	○	○				●	●	●	●		●
Essex																								
Drama ①	○	○	○	○	○	●	●	●																
Exeter																								
Drama	●	●	●	○	○	●	●	○	○					○	○				○					

Course content

Key: O optional; ● compulsory; ◐ compulsory + options
① ⓘ : see notes after table

Institution / Course title	Performance	Directing	Production	Stage design	Stage/studio management	History of theatre or dance	Textual analysis	Scriptwriting	Radio	Television	Film	Video	Wardrobe/make-up	Drama/dance in the community	Drama/dance in education	Administration	Mime	Ballet	Contemporary dance	Jazz dance	Non-Western/other dance styles	Choreography	Dance notation	Dance analysis
Glamorgan																								
Drama (theatre and media)	O	O	O	O	O	O	●	O	O	O	O	O				O								
Glasgow																								
Theatre studies ①	O	O	O	O	O	●	●	O						O	O	O								
Goldsmiths																								
Drama and theatre arts	◐	◐	●	◐	◐	●	O				◐	O	O	◐	O	O					O			
Guildhall S Music & Drama																								
Acting ①	●					●	●	●	●	●		●					●							
Huddersfield																								
Drama ①	●	O	O	◐	◐	●	O	O	O					◐	O				O		O			
Hull																								
Drama	O	O	O	O	O	●	◐	O	O					O	O	O								
Theatre and performance studies ①	●	O	O	O	O	●	●				O			O	O	O								
Kent																								
Drama and theatre studies ①	O	O	O	O	O	O	O							O	O	O								
Kingston																								
Drama	◐	O	●			●	O	O	O	O	O	O				●					O			
Laban																								
Dance theatre ①	●	O												O	O	O			●	●		●	●	●
Leeds																								
Dance	●	●	●										◐	●					●			●		●
English literature and theatre studies	O	O	●		O	O	●				O	O	O	O	O	O								
Lincoln																								
Drama		●		●	●		●									●								
Liverpool Hope																								
Creative and performing arts ①	●	O	O		O		O							◐	O	●			O	O		O		
Drama and theatre studies	O	O	O	O	O	O	O								O				O		O	O	O	
LIPA																								
Acting (performing arts) ①	●	O				●	●	●		●	●	●	◐	◐		◐	◐		●	●	◐			
Dance (performing arts)	●		●			●	●			O	O			O	O	◐	◐	●	●	●	◐			
Liverpool John Moores																								
Dance studies	◐	●		●		●	●				●			◐	◐	◐		◐	●	O		◐	◐	◐
Drama	◐	◐	◐	O		◐	O												O					
London Metropolitan																								
Theatre studies	O	O	O		◐	●		O																
Loughborough																								
Drama ①	●	O	O		O	●	●	O	O	O	O			O	O	O								
Manchester																								
Drama	O	O				●	●			O	●			O	O									
Manchester Metropolitan																								
Acting	●					●	●		●	●	●										●			
Contemporary theatre and performance	●	O	◐	O	O	◐	◐					O												
Dance	◐																		◐	◐		◐	◐	◐
Drama	◐	◐	◐		O		◐	O		O	O			O	O				O					
Marjon																								
Drama	●	O	O	O	O	●	●	O	O	O	O	O		●	●	O	O		O		O			
Middlesex																								
Dance performance	●				●							O		◐				●	●	●	O	●		●
Dance studies	●			O								O		●				●	●	O	O	●		●

Drama and Dance

(continued) Table 3a

Course content

○ optional; ● compulsory; ◑ compulsory + options
① ② : see notes after table

Institution / Course title	Performance	Directing	Production	Stage design	Stage/studio management	History of theatre or dance	Textual analysis	Scriptwriting	Radio	Television	Film	Video	Wardrobe/make-up	Drama/dance in the community	Drama/dance in education	Administration	Mime	Ballet	Contemporary dance	Jazz dance	Non-Western/other dance styles	Choreography	Dance notation	Dance analysis
Middlesex (continued)																								
Dance with performing arts	●	○	○	○	○							○		○				●	●	○	○	●		●
Drama and theatre arts	◑	◑	●	◑	◑	●	●	○		○			◑	◑	○	◑								
Newman C																								
Drama	◑	○	◑	◑	◑	○	◑	◑						◑	◑									
Northampton																								
Dance	◑		◑	○	○						○			○	○	○		○	◑		○	◑		○
Drama	●	●	●	●	●	●	●						●	●		●								
Performance	●	●	●	●	●	●	●						●	●		●						●	●	
Northumbria																								
Dance/choreography	●	○	●	●	●							●	○	●	●				●	●	●	●		●
Drama	●	○	○	●	○	●	●	○	○	○	○		●	●	●				●					
Performance ①	●	○	○	●	○	●	●	○	○	●	●		●	●	○				●	○	○			
Peterborough RC																								
Performing arts ①	●		●	●	●	●	●							●	●	◑								
Plymouth																								
Theatre and performance ①	●	○	○			○	●	○					○	●		○						●	●	○
Portsmouth																								
Drama	○	○	○	○		○		○	○	○	○		○											
Queen Margaret																								
Acting and performance ①	●					●	●		●	●	●													
Drama and theatre arts ②	●	○	◑		○		○							○	○									
Queen Mary																								
Drama ①	○				○																			
Reading																								
Film and theatre	◑	◑	◑	◑	◑	●	●	◑		◑	●	●												
Roehampton																								
Dance studies	●					●	◑			◑	◑	◑		○	○		○	○	●			●	◑	
Drama and theatre studies	●	○	○	○	○	○	●	○							○									
Rose Bruford C																								
Acting	●					●	●		●	●	●													
Actor-musician ①	●					●	○		●	●	●		●											
Directing	●	●	●	●	●	●	●		●	●														
European/American theatre arts	●	●	●	●	●	●	○							○	○	○						○		
Royal Holloway																								
Drama and theatre studies ①	◑	◑	◑	◑	◑	◑	◑	◑		○	○	○	◑	○					○			○	○	○
International theatre (Australia/France) ②	○	○	○	○	○	●	●	○						○	○									○
Royal Scottish A Music & Drama																								
Contemporary theatre practice	●	●	●	●		●	●				○			●	●	◑			○			●		
Royal Welsh C Music & Drama																								
Acting	●					●	●		●		●								●	●				
St Martin's C																								
Drama	○	○	○	○	○								○	●	●	○			○		○			
St Mary's C																								
Drama and performance studies ①	○	○	○	○	○		●	○		○			○	○	○				○		○			
Physical theatre ②	●	○	○	○	○	●	●	○					○	○	○	◑	○	◑	○	◑	○	○	○	◑
Staffordshire																								
Theatre arts	●		◑		◑	◑	◑	○	○	○	○													

Course content

Institution / Course title ①②: see notes after table	optional ○; compulsory ●; compulsory + options ◐	Performance	Directing	Production	Stage design	Stage/studio management	History of theatre or dance	Textual analysis	Scriptwriting	Radio	Television	Film	Video	Wardrobe/make-up	Drama/dance in the community	Drama/dance in education	Administration	Mime	Ballet	Contemporary dance	Jazz dance	Non-Western/other dance styles	Choreography	Dance notation	Dance analysis
Surrey Dance and culture		◐				◐					○	○	○		○	○	○		◐	◐		◐	◐	◐	◐
Swansea IHE Performing arts and theatre studies		●	○	●		○	●	●																	
Trinity C (Carmarthen) Theatre studies		●	○	○	○	○	●	●							○	○	○			○		○	○	○	○
UC Suffolk Performing arts		●	●	●	◐	◐	●	●	●					◐	◐	◐			●			●			
UCE Birmingham English and drama ①		◐					●	●	●	○															
Ulster Drama		◐	○	○	○	○	●	●	○		○	○			○	○	○								
University of the Arts London Acting		●			●		●	●			●	●		●				●	●						
Wales (UWIC) Dance ①		●				●									●	●	●			●		●	●	●	●
Warwick Theatre and performance studies			○	○			●	●				○			○	○	○								
Winchester Choreography and dance studies ①		◐		◐		●					○				●	●			○	●		●		●	
Drama		●	○	●	○	○	○	●							○	○	○								
Drama, community theatre and media		●		●			●	●			●	●	●		●	●	●								
Performing arts ②		●	●	●	◐	○	●	●	●	●	◐	◐	◐	○	◐	○	○	◐	○	●		●	◐		●
Wolverhampton Dance practice and performance		●		●	○						○	○	○	○	○			◐	●	○	○				●
Drama and performance		◐	○	◐	○	○	●	●	○	○	○	○	○		○	○	○								
Worcester Drama and performance studies ①		◐	○	○	○		●	●	○		○				○	○	○			○					○
York St John Performance: dance		●	○	●	◐	●					○	○			●	●	○						●	○	●
Performance: theatre		●	●	●	○	○	●	●	○	○	○	●	○		●	●	◐						○	○	○
Theatre ①		●	●	●	○	○	●	●	◐		●	●		○	○	○	●								

Aberystwyth ① Analysis of space; lighting/sound design; inter-cultural theatre ② Devising performance; performance writing
Anglia Ruskin ① Devising
Bath Spa ① Dance and sound/visual arts/text
Brighton ① Range of topics in visual arts and art and performance history; installation; lighting ② Installation; scenography; lighting design
Bristol ① Performance theory; critical analyses of performance projects
Bristol UWE ① 19th and 20th C British, European and American drama
Brunel ① Cultural context of performance
Central Lancashire ① Voice; movement ② Theory ③ Movement; music composition and performance; voice

Chichester ① Dance and technology; repertory; dance movement therapy
Coventry ① Cultural studies ② Contemporary performance; adaptation; physical theatre
De Montfort ① History of dance ② Arts funding training
East London ① Lighting for performance
Edge Hill ① Dance and technology
Essex ① Comedy
Glasgow ① Performance analysis; cultural policy
Guildhall S Music & Drama ① Improvisation
Huddersfield ① Physical theatre; carnival; commedia dell'arte
Hull ① Lighting design; scenography; politics and performance; theatre and culture; devising
Kent ① Computer-aided design

Drama and Dance

Laban ① Dance culture; repertory; music; aesthetics; professional studies
Liverpool Hope ① Wide range of topics and activities in music and visual arts; documentary theatre; theatre making
LIPA ① Voice and movement; musical theatre; professional development; information and performance technology
Loughborough ① Theoretical analysis
Northumbria ① Music theatre; physical theatre
Peterborough RC ① Touring for small-scale theatre; professional practice
Plymouth ① Cross-cultural studies
Queen Margaret ① Ballroom dance; historical movement and dance; jazz; stage combat; singing; improvisation; presentation (auditions) ② Literary management; media criticism; contemporary performance

Queen Mary ① Applied theatre
Rose Bruford C ① Musical performance as actor and musician
Royal Holloway ① World theatre; lighting and sound; costume design; new technologies and theatre ② French language and drama
St Mary's C ① Design options in lighting, costume and scenic design ② Performance analysis
UCE Birmingham ① Theatre criticism
Wales (UWIC) ① Dance pedagogy/leadership
Winchester ① Dance criticism; performance and sexuality ② Interdisciplinarity; music skills; improvising and devising
Worcester ① Theatre reviewing; gender and theatre; physical theatre; theatre and disability; managing a theatre company
York St John ① 20th C literature studies; literary adaptations; 'fictions'

Practical activities   TABLE 3b shows how the balance between practical and other activities varies between courses and as each course progresses. It also gives brief details of some of the practical activities on offer.

Institution	Course title	First year: minimum/maximum %	Intermediate year(s): minimum/maximum %	Final year: minimum/maximum %	Other practical activities
Aberystwyth	Drama	20/40	20/40	40/60	
	Performance studies	25/25	40/50	40/50	Solo/group presentations; performance fragments; performance etudes
Anglia Ruskin	Drama	17/42	25/59	25/59	Independent performance projects; large-scale public performances; small-scale theatre performances; TV drama production and workshop
Arts Institute at Bournemouth	Acting for theatre, film and television	65	65	65	Year 1: actor's practical tools and skills; years 2 and 3: production opportunities as preparation for professional life
Bangor	Theatre studies	10/20	30/50	50/70	
Bath Spa	Dance	50/75	50/75	50/75	Choreography for solo, duet and small-group dance; choreographic research project
	Performing arts	60/100	70/100	90/100	
Birmingham	Drama and theatre arts	60/60	50/50	50/50	
Bishop Grosseteste C	Drama in the community	70/70	70/70	50/75	Practical project in the community, negotiated, planned and implemented by individual students
Brighton	Dance and visual art	80/80	80/80	60/80	Improvisation; installation; performance composition using live and virtual body
	Theatre and visual art	80/80	80/80	60/80	Site-specific performance; composition/performance; installation; tape/slide; photography

Practical work

Practical work

Institution	Course title	First year: minimum/maximum %	Intermediate year(s): minimum/maximum %	Final year: minimum/maximum %	Other practical activities
Bristol	Drama	55/**55**	55/**55**	55/**55**	Theatre productions and workshops, TV studio production; single camera video-making; installation (live and filmed)
Bristol UWE	Drama	25/**30**	25/**25**	25/**25**	
Brunel	Modern drama studies	33/**66**	35/**65**	35/**75**	Text-based and devised work; experimental performance
Buckinghamshire Chilterns UC	Drama	50/**50**	50/**50**	50/**50**	
Central Lancashire	Acting	80/**80**	80/**80**	80/**80**	Productions and performances
	English and theatre studies	33/**33**	33/**33**	33/**50**	
	Music theatre	80/**80**	80/**80**	80/**80**	Composition/instrumental and voice/movement pathways
	Theatre practice	80/**80**	80/**80**	80/**80**	Devising and performing; text-based theatre; dance and physical theatre
Chester	*Both courses*	50/**75**	25/**75**	25/**75**	
Chichester	Dance	77/**88**	72/**83**	55/**72**	Ballet technique; contact improvisation; performance in other students' choreography; video dances; contemporary dance; dance production; dance in the community
	Performing arts	60/**60**	60/**75**	60/**80**	Devised theatre; touring in the community; voice work; movement; directing; video drama; music theatre
City C Manchester	Acting studies	**100**	**100**	**100**	
Coventry	Dance and professional practice	60/**60**	70/**70**	50/**60**	Performance projects; collaborative projects; practical dance techniques; fitness work
	Theatre and professional practice	63/**63**	75/**75**	50/**60**	Performance projects; collaborative projects; acting sessions incorporating voice and movement
Cumbria I	Performing arts	60/**80**	60/**80**	60/**80**	
De Montfort	Dance	50/**75**	50/**75**	50/**75**	
	Performing arts	60/**60**		70/**70**	Active technique/dance technique; sound/lighting design; interdisciplinary performance work; workshop planning and facilitation
Derby	Theatre studies	100/**100**	100/**100**	100/**100**	Theatre in education project; theatre workshops
East Anglia	Drama	30/**50**	30/**50**	30/**50**	Assessed group production, involving rehearsal, performance and technical work; practical classes eg technical, voice, movement; option of practical professional placement in year 2
Edge Hill	Drama	50/**60**	50/**65**	50/**70**	Performance; tutor- and student-directed productions; design of sets and costumes; creation of performance texts; work in schools/community
	Drama, physical theatre and dance	50/**60**	50/**65**	50/**70**	Performance; tutor- and student-directed productions in drama, dance and physical theatre; creation of performance texts; work in schools/community
Essex	Drama	**30**	**30**	**30**	Year 1: optional course in technical theatre; year 3: theatre writing course (students write 15-minute play)

Practical work

Institution	Course title	First year: minimum/maximum %	Intermediate year(s): minimum/maximum %	Final year: minimum/maximum %	Other practical activities
Exeter	Drama	60/**75**	75/**75**	50/**75**	
Glamorgan	Drama (theatre and media)	30/**80**	30/**80**	40/**80**	
Glasgow	Theatre studies	**0**	0/**20**	0/**20**	
Goldsmiths	Drama and theatre arts	50/**60**	40/**60**	25/**75**	Year 1 directing exercise, using selected theatrical elements of light, sound and costume; years 2 and 3 performance projects
	English and drama	7/**12**	**0**	**0**	
Guildhall S Music & Drama	Acting	60	70	80	Rehearsal; public performances
Huddersfield	Drama	55/**75**	60/**70**	50/**75**	Practical electives taught by professionals (dance, directing, lighting etc)
Hull	Drama	40/**60**	40/**60**	40/**60**	Concentrated production assignments
	Theatre and performance studies	50/**60**	40/**70**	40/**70**	Theatre-based work placements; workshop and production projects
Kent	Drama and theatre studies	40/**40**	50/**50**	80/**80**	Devised theatre; community celebration; radio production
Kingston	Drama	30/**100**	30/**100**	30/**100**	Workshops; rehearsals; devised presentations; scripted presentations; play productions; performance essays
Laban	Dance theatre	90/**90**	90/**90**	90/**90**	Improvisation; Pilates; collaborative project; performance workshop
Leeds	Dance	70	60	50	Technique class; choreographic workshops
	English literature and theatre studies	12/**17**	20/**33**	35/**50**	Production workshops (years 2 and 3); devised theatre project (year 3)
Liverpool Hope	Creative and performing arts	25/**50**	40/**60**	40/**60**	
	Drama and theatre studies	50/**50**	50/**50**	33/**66**	
LIPA	Acting (performing arts)	80/**80**	80/**80**	80/**80**	Performance workshops; collaborative performance; public performance projects; recorded performances
	Dance (performing arts)	80/**80**	80/**80**	40/**70**	Pilates/body conditioning; musical theatre; collaborative projects
Liverpool John Moores	Dance studies	50/**70**	40/**80**	40/**80**	Technique; teaching; physical theatre
	Drama				Full-scale productions (year 3)
London Metropolitan	Theatre studies	15/**20**	0/**20**	0/**20**	Workshop-based practical activities
Loughborough	Drama	25/**50**	40/**60**	40/**60**	
Manchester	Drama	40/**60**	40/**60**	30/**40**	Practical presentation of research; video-making; devising (for education, prisons etc)
Manchester Metropolitan	Acting	90/**100**	100	100	
	Contemporary theatre and performance	60/**70**	50/**70**	50/**70**	
	Dance	60/**60**	30/**70**	30/**70**	
	Drama	60/**60**	30/**70**	30/**70**	
Marjon	Drama	25/**75**	30/**75**	50/**50**	Projects/placements with Barefoot Project (professional arts organisation on campus)
Middlesex	Dance performance	50/**75**	50/**75**	50/**75**	Dance techniques including Graham-based, Cunningham-based, Humphrey-based, Release-based; fitness for dance; structural fitness; choreography

Practical work

Institution	Course title	First year: minimum/maximum %	Intermediate year(s): minimum/maximum %	Final year: minimum/maximum %	Other practical activities
Middlesex (continued)	Dance studies	50/75	50/75	50/75	Dance techniques including Graham-based, Cunningham-based, Humphrey-based, Release-based; fitness for dance; structural fitness; choreography
	Dance with performing arts	50/75	50/75	50/75	Dance techniques including Graham-based, Cunningham-based, Humphrey-based, Release-based; fitness for dance; choreography
	Drama and theatre arts	20/60	20/60	20/60	Group production work, including performance, directing, devising, design and technical operation; workshop exploration of key practitioners, texts and processes
Northampton	Dance	50/80	60/90	50/80	Creating and performing choreographies; 2 dance techniques (including Release-based); placements in established organisations and companies
	Drama	70/70	70/70	70/70	
	Performance	55	55	55	Community performance; music theatre
Northumbria	*All courses*	75/75	75/75	75/75	
Peterborough RC	Performing arts	50/60	50/60	40/60	Voice acting; voice singing; devising and performing; creative movement and performance art; technical theatre
Plymouth	Theatre and performance	**60**	**60**	**60**	
Portsmouth	Drama	40/40	40/40	40/40	
Queen Margaret	Acting and performance	95	95	95	
	Drama and theatre arts	30/35	33/42	25/40	Devising; making theatre; skills performance
Queen Mary	Drama	50	50	50	
Reading	Film and theatre	33/33	25/25	0/25	Practical film, video, theatre direction options in years 2 and 3
Roehampton	Dance studies	55/85	60/85	60/75	
	Drama and theatre studies	20/40	20/40	20/40	
Rose Bruford C	Acting	80/85	80/85	80/85	
	Actor-musician	80/85	80/85	80/85	Includes musical direction, composition and instrumental performance
	Directing	80/85	70/85	70/85	
	European/American theatre arts	50/70	50/70	50/70	American theatre arts: most of year 2 at SFA University, Texas; European theatre arts: part of year 2 in European theatre companies
Royal Holloway	Drama and theatre studies	30/30	20/80	20/80	Optional whole term on production project
	International theatre (Australia/France)	10/50	10/50	10/50	
Royal Scottish A Music & Drama	Contemporary theatre practice	20/80	20/80	20/80	Work placement
Royal Welsh C Music & Drama	Acting	**80**	**80**	**80**	Professional vocational course
St Martin's C	Drama	50/55	50/65	50/65	
St Mary's C	Drama and performance studies	75/75	25/60	25/60	Performance; directing; technical theatre; design; playwriting
	Physical theatre	50/80	50/80	50/80	

Drama and Dance

67

Institution	Course title	First year: minimum/maximum %	Intermediate year(s): minimum/maximum %	Final year: minimum/maximum %	Other practical activities
	Practical work				
Staffordshire	Theatre arts	40/50	60/70	30/70	Performing Shakespeare; devised work; documentary drama; live art performances; playwriting; placements at local theatres and schools
Surrey	Dance and culture	66/66	50/60	0/60	African peoples' dance; Kathak; Pilates and fitness programme; documentation and reconstruction; ballet; contemporary dance
Swansea IHE	Performing arts and theatre studies	25	25	25	Practical theatre projects, including complete play performances
Trinity C (Carmarthen)	Theatre studies	50/50	33/67	33/67	
UC Suffolk	Performing arts	17/83	33/66	50/50	Performance techniques; public productions; technical theatre; self-devising
UCE Birmingham	English and drama	20/40	30/50	30/50	Scripting workshops; devising; rehearsal techniques
Ulster	Drama	40/50	15/50	15/50	
University of the Arts London	Acting	25/33	25/33	55/70	
Wales (UWIC)	Dance	50/60	50/60	50/60	Ballet; jazz; contemporary dance; choreographic research; dance pedagogy
Warwick	Theatre and performance studies	25/25	25/50	25	Workshops on performance, community theatre video
Winchester	Choreography and dance studies	50/70	30/70	30/70	
	Drama	50/75	50/50	40/60	Seminar presentations; devised group performance project
	Drama, community theatre and media	40/60	40/60	40/60	Community drama; video documentary
	Performing arts	50/70	40/60	40/60	
Wolverhampton	Dance practice and performance	40/70	40/70	40/70	
	Drama and performance	60	75	75	Group practical performed in university or in school/community venues
Worcester	Drama and performance studies	50/50	50/60	40/80	Full public performance; devised performance; dance and physical theatre
York St John	Performance: dance	40/60	40/60	40/60	
	Performance: theatre	65/85	65/85	65/85	Experimental theatre and live art; theatre placements
	Theatre	50/70	50/70	50/80	Work placements with theatres and in TV/video production; video and theatre production for outside clients; European and US exchanges; internship programmes with theatre, film and TV companies in year 3

Chapter 4: Assessment methods

For general information on assessment, see Chapter 4 in the first part of this Guide. TABLE 4 shows the assessment methods in use in drama and dance courses.

Table 4

Assessment methods

Institution	Course title	Key for frequency of assessment column: ● term; ◐ semester; ○ year / Frequency of assessment	Years of exams contributing to final degree (years of exams not contributing to final degree)	Coursework: minimum/maximum %	Project/dissertation: minimum/maximum %
Aberystwyth	Drama	◐	(1),2,3	20/50	20/50
	Performance studies	◐	(1),2,3	50/50	50/50
Anglia Ruskin	Drama	◐	(1),2,3	40/83	17/60
Arts Institute at Bournemouth	Acting for theatre, film and television	◑		20/20	80/80
Bangor	Theatre studies	◐	(1),2,3	50	15
Bath Spa	Dance	◐		25/50	50/75
	Drama studies	◑		30/70	30/70
	Performing arts	◐			80/100
Birmingham	Drama and theatre arts	◐		80/80	20/20
Bishop Grosseteste C	Drama in the community	◐		0/20	40/80
Brighton	Dance and visual art	◑		60/80	20/40
	Theatre and visual art	◑			80/80
Bristol	Drama	◑		25/60	40/75
Bristol UWE	Drama	◑	(1),2,3	37/45	12/25
Brunel	Modern drama studies	◐	(1),2	20/80	20/80
Buckinghamshire Chilterns UC	Drama	◐	(1),2,3	75/75	25/25
Central Lancashire	Acting	◐		80/80	20/20
	English and theatre studies	◐	(1),2,3	50/66	34/50
	Music theatre	◐		20/20	80/80
	Theatre practice	◐		80	20
Chester	*Both courses*	◐	2,3	25/75	10/75
Chichester	Dance	◐	(1),2	80/80	20/20
	Performing arts	◐	(1)	80	20
City C Manchester	Acting studies	◑			
Coventry	Dance and professional practice	◑		40/50	50/60
	Theatre and professional practice	◑		40/50	50/60
Cumbria I	Dance			60	40
	Drama			60	40
	Music theatre			60	40
	Performing arts	◑		60	40
Dartington CA	Theatre	◐			
De Montfort	Dance	○		75/88	12/25
	Drama studies	○	(1),2,3	50/75	12/25
	Performing arts	◑		30	70
Derby	Theatre studies	◐		75/100	
East Anglia	Drama	◐			
Edge Hill	Drama	◐		60/60	40/40
	Drama, physical theatre and dance			60/60	40/40
Essex	Drama	◑	(1),2,3	40/50	**12**

Drama and Dance

Assessment methods

Institution	Course title	Frequency of assessment	Years of exams contributing to final degree (years of exams not contributing to final degree)	Coursework: minimum/maximum %	Project/dissertation: minimum/maximum %
Exeter	Drama	◐	(1),**2,3**	75/**90**	10/**25**
Glamorgan	Drama (theatre and media)	◐	(1),(2),**3**	40/**60**	0/**20**
Glasgow	Theatre studies	◐●	(1),(2),**4**	30/**30**	20/**20**
Goldsmiths	Drama and theatre arts	◐●	**1**	25/**75**	25/**75**
	English and drama		**1,2,3**	40/**70**	20
Guildhall S Music & Drama	Acting	◐●		52/**52**	15/**15**
Huddersfield	Drama	◐	(1),**2,3**	25/**60**	40/**75**
Hull	Drama	◐	(1),**2**	70/**80**	20/**25**
	Theatre and performance studies	◐		50/**75**	25/**50**
Kent	Drama and theatre studies	○	(1),**2,3**	50/**50**	33/**45**
Kingston	Drama	◐			
Laban	Dance theatre	◐●		75/**75**	25/**25**
Leeds	Dance	◐	(1),(2),(3)	**50**	**50**
	English literature and theatre studies	◐	(1),**2,3**	33/**66**	0/**8**
Lincoln	Drama	◐	**1,2,3**		
Liverpool Hope	Creative and performing arts	◐	(1),**2**	40/**50**	40/**60**
	Drama and theatre studies	◐	(1),**2**,(3)	50/**100**	0/**50**
LIPA	Acting (performing arts)	◐●		40/**60**	20/**40**
	Dance (performing arts)	◐●		40/**60**	20/**60**
Liverpool John Moores	Dance studies	◐	(1),**2**	25/**60**	40/**75**
	Drama	◐	(1),**2,3**		
London Metropolitan	Theatre studies	◐		100	
Loughborough	Drama	◐	(1),**2,3**	25/**25**	75/**75**
Manchester	Drama		**1,2,3**	40/**60**	40/**60**
Manchester Metropolitan	Acting	◐●		70/**70**	30/**30**
	Contemporary theatre and performance	◐●			
	Dance	◐●		40/**70**	30/**60**
	Drama	◐●		40/**70**	30/**60**
Marjon	Drama	◐●		40/**60**	30/**70**
Middlesex	Dance performance	◐		50	50
	Dance studies	◐		50	50
	Dance with performing arts	◐		50	50
	Drama and theatre arts	◐		90/**95**	5/**10**
Newman C	Drama	◐●	(1),**2,3**		
Northampton	Dance	○	(1),**2,3**	74/**87**	13/**26**
	Drama		(1),**2,3**	10/**10**	13/**26**
	Performance	◐	(1),**2,3**	85/**87**	13/**13**
Northumbria	Dance/choreography	◐		**75**	**75**
	Drama	◐	**1,2,3**	60/**60**	40/**40**
	Performance	◐		**50**	**50**
Peterborough RC	Performing arts	◐	(2)	76/**76**	24/**24**
Plymouth	Theatre and performance	◐		**35**	**65**
Portsmouth	Drama	◐	(1),**2,3**	70/**70**	30/**30**
Queen Margaret	Acting and performance	◐	**4**	90	10
	Drama and theatre arts	◐	(1),(2)	**66**	**33**
Queen Mary	Drama	◐	**1,2,3,4**	90/**90**	10/**10**

Assessment methods

Institution	Course title	Key for frequency of assessment column: ● term; ◑ semester; ○ year / Frequency of assessment	Years of exams contributing to final degree (years of exams not contributing to final degree)	Coursework: minimum/maximum %	Project/dissertation: minimum/maximum %
Reading	Film and theatre	◐	(1),3	50/50	10/10
Roehampton	Dance studies	◑	(1),2,3	60/60	20/40
	Drama and theatre studies	◑	(1),2,3	60/80	20/20
Rose Bruford C	Acting	◑		75/75	25/25
	Actor-musician	◐		75/75	25/25
	Directing			75/75	25/25
	European/American theatre arts	◐		50/50	50/50
Royal Holloway	Drama and theatre studies	◐	(1)	50/90	10/50
	International theatre (Australia/France)	◑	(1),2		
Royal Scottish A Music & Drama	Contemporary theatre practice	◐	(1),(2),(3),(4)		100
Royal Welsh C Music & Drama	Acting	◐		30/30	70/70
St Martin's C	Drama	◐	(1),2,3	45/55	5/10
St Mary's C	Drama and performance studies	◑	(1),2,3	25/75	0/50
	Physical theatre	◑	(1),2	40/50	50/60
Staffordshire	Theatre arts	◑		70/70	30/30
Surrey	Dance and culture	◑	(1),2,3,4	60/60	40/40
Swansea IHE	Performing arts and theatre studies	◑		50/50	50/50
Trinity C (Carmarthen)	Theatre studies	◑	(1),3	33/33	33/67
UC Suffolk	Performing arts	◑	(1),(2),(3)	17/34	66/83
UCE Birmingham	English and drama	◑		80/100	0/20
Ulster	Drama	◑	(1),3	62/75	12/12
University of the Arts London	Acting	◐	(1),(2),(3)	100/100	
Wales (UWIC)	Dance	◐	(1),2	40/45	50/60
Warwick	Theatre and performance studies	◐	(1),2,3	65	
Winchester	Choreography and dance studies	◑	2,3	100/100	
	Drama	◑	(1),2,3		
	Drama, community theatre and media	◑	(1),2,3	30/50	20/20
	Performing arts	◑	(1),2,3	40/60	20/60
Wolverhampton	Dance practice and performance	◑	(1),2,3	60/70	30/40
	Drama and performance	◑	(1),2,3	40/40	12/25
Worcester	Drama and performance studies	◑	(1),2,3	80/100	0/20
York St John	Performance: dance	◑		50/50	50/50
	Performance: theatre	◑		30/30	70/70
	Theatre	◑		80/90	10/20

Drama and Dance

For general information on entrance requirements, see Chapter 5 in the first part of this Guide; note that four institutions (ALRA, Guildhall School of Music and Drama, Laban and Royal Scottish Academy of Music and Drama) take applications directly, rather than through UCAS: for these, use the address at the end of this Guide or the website given in TABLE 2a. TABLE 5 shows the entrance requirements for courses in drama and dance, as well as student numbers for each course. The table also shows whether an audition or other practical test is required as well as, or instead of, the usual A-level requirements.

Table 5 — Entrance requirements

Institution	Course title	Number of students (includes other courses)	Typical offers: UCAS tariff points	A-levels	SCQF Highers	● compulsory; O preferred	A-level Theatre studies	A-level Dance	Practical test
Aberystwyth	Drama	80	280				O		
	Performance studies	30	280				O		
Anglia Ruskin	Drama		200–240		BBCC	●			
Arts Institute at Bournemouth	Acting for theatre, film and television	30	160				O		●
Bangor	Theatre studies	10	200–240		BBCC				
Bath Spa	Dance	59	200–240				O	O	●
	Drama studies	120	200–240				O		●
	Performing arts	40	180–200				O		●
Birmingham	Drama and theatre arts	40	320	AAB	AABBB		O		●
Bishop Grosseteste C	Drama in the community	22	140				O		●
Brighton	Dance and visual art	21						O	●
	Theatre and visual art	23					O	O	
Bristol	Drama	30	300	BBB	AAABB		O		●
Bristol UWE	Drama	100	240–300				O		
Brunel	Modern drama studies	60	280		BBBBC		O	O	
Buckinghamshire Chilterns UC	Drama	40	120–240		CCCC		O		
Central Lancashire	Acting	25	240				O	O	●
	English and theatre studies	10	220		BBBC		O		
	Music theatre	25	260				O	O	●
	Theatre practice	25	180		BCCC		O	O	●
Chester	Dance		280	CCC	BBBB		O	O	●
	Drama and theatre studies		240–260	CCC	BBBB		O	O	●
Chichester	Dance	50	220–240					O	●
	Performing arts	50	240–280				O	O	●
City C Manchester	Acting studies	30	80–160				O		●
Coventry	Dance and professional practice	30	200–220					O	●
	Theatre and professional practice	30	200–220				O		●
Cumbria I	Dance	20	160	BB	ABB			O	●
	Drama	20	160	BB	ABB				●
	Music theatre	20	160	CC	BBC				●
	Performing arts	40	160	BB	ABB	O			●

(continued) Table 5

Entrance requirements

Institution	Course title	Number of students (includes other courses)	UCAS tariff points	A-levels	SCQF Highers	A-level Theatre studies	A-level Dance	Practical test
De Montfort	Dance	58	180–200		BBBB			●
	Drama studies	40	220		BBBB			●
	Performing arts	44	180					
Derby	Theatre studies	55	140–160			○		
East Anglia	Drama	18	300–320	BBB		○		●
East London	Performing arts		160					
Edge Hill	Drama	45	240			○		
	Drama, physical theatre and dance	45	240				○	
Essex	Drama	35	300	BB	BBBB			●
Exeter	Drama	113	280–360	AAA				
Glamorgan	Drama (theatre and media)	40	200–240			○		
Glasgow	Theatre studies	(130)		ABB	BBBB			
Goldsmiths	Drama and theatre arts	55		BBB	BBBBB	○		
	English and drama	20		BBB	BBBBB			
Guildhall S Music & Drama	Acting	25		EE				●
Huddersfield	Drama	45	240		BBBC	○		●
Hull	Drama	50		BBB	AABBB			
	Theatre and performance studies	50	240		BBBB	○		
Kent	Drama and theatre studies		260–280			○		
Kingston	Drama	35	280–320					
Laban	Dance theatre	90		CC			○	●
Leeds	Dance	40	260	BBC			○	●
	English literature and theatre studies	18	240	AAB				
Lincoln	Drama	36	220					●
Liverpool Hope	Creative and performing arts		220					
	Drama and theatre studies		220					
LIPA	Acting (performing arts)	30	180					●
	Dance (performing arts)	22	180				○	●
Liverpool John Moores	Dance studies	40	160				○	
	Drama	40	180–240	BBC	BBBC	●		●
London Metropolitan	Performing arts		160		CCCC			●
	Theatre studies	40	160			○		
London South Bank	Acting	30		CC	BBB	○	○	●
Loughborough	Drama	55	320			○		
Manchester	Drama	65		AAB	AABBB			
Manchester Metropolitan	Acting	24	80–240		BBB	○		●
	Contemporary theatre and performance	25	200		CCC	○		●
	Dance	30	200		BBB		○	●
	Drama	80	200		BBB	○		●
Marjon	Drama	16	140–200					
Middlesex	Dance performance	35	160–280	CC			○	●
	Dance studies	20	160–280	CC			○	●
	Dance with performing arts	15	160–280	CC			○	●
	Drama and theatre arts	85	160–280					●
Newman C	Drama	20	160		CCC	○		

● compulsory, ○ preferred

Drama and Dance

Institution	Course title	Number of students (includes other courses)	UCAS tariff points	A-levels	SCQF Highers	● compulsory; ○ preferred A-level Theatre studies	A-level Dance	Practical test
Northampton	Dance	25	180–220		BBCC		○	●
	Drama	40	180–220		BBCC	○		
	Performance	30	180–220		BBCC	○	○	
Northumbria	Dance/choreography	25	260		BBCCC			●
	Drama	30	260	BCC	BBCCC			●
	Performance	30	260	BCC	BBCCC			●
Peterborough RC	Performing arts	15	120–360					
Plymouth	Theatre and performance	50	220			○	○	●
Portsmouth	Drama	20	240–300					
Queen Margaret	Acting and performance	22		EE	CCC			●
	Drama and theatre arts	36	280	BBC	ABBCC	○		
Queen Mary	Drama	30	300–370		AABBB			●
Reading	Film and theatre	25	300–340			○		
Roehampton	Dance studies	50	280				○	●
	Drama and theatre studies	70	260			○		
Rose Bruford C	Acting	23	160–280					●
	Actor-musician	15	160–280					●
	Directing	10	200–280					●
	European/American theatre arts	23	200–280					●
Royal Holloway	Drama and theatre studies	75	320–340			○		●
	International theatre (Australia/France)	(65)	320–340			○		
Royal Scottish A Music & Drama	Contemporary theatre practice	16						●
Royal Welsh C Music & Drama	Acting	20	120–200			○		●
St Martin's C	Drama	40	200	CC	BBCC			●
St Mary's C	Drama and performance studies	120	160–200	BB		○		●
	Physical theatre	60	160–200	CC		○	○	●
Salford	Performing arts		240		BBBBC			●
Staffordshire	Theatre arts	40	160–200		BBC			
Surrey	Dance and culture	47	280–300	BBB	BBBCC		○	●
Swansea IHE	Performing arts and theatre studies		160–340					
Thames Valley	Drama: acting for stage and media		160		BCC			
Trinity C (Carmarthen)	Theatre studies	(50)	120–360			○		
UC Suffolk	Performing arts	18	120–180			○	○	●
UCE Birmingham	English and drama		200					
Ulster	Drama	20	240					●
University of the Arts London	Acting	32				○		●
Wales (UWIC)	Dance	23		BB		○	○	●
Warwick	Theatre and performance studies	35		ABB		○		
Winchester	Choreography and dance studies	40	240			○	○	
	Drama	50	260					
	Drama, community theatre and media	36	260					
	Performing arts	120	260			○	○	●
Wolverhampton	Dance practice and performance	40	160–220				○	●
	Drama and performance	50	160–220					●
Worcester	Drama and performance studies	60	160			○		

Institution	Course title	Number of students (includes other courses)	Typical offers	UCAS tariff points	A-levels	SCQF Highers	● compulsory; ○ preferred	A-level Theatre studies	A-level Dance	Practical test
York St John	Performance: dance	20	160			BBC		○	○	●
	Performance: theatre	40	160			BBC		○		●
	Theatre	80	160			BBC		○		●

Entrance requirements

Background information   Chapter 6 of the first part of this Guide contains a list of publications containing information about admission to higher education, financial support and access for special groups of applicants.

Other useful information and addresses

Association of Dance Movement Therapy UK 32 Meadfoot Lane, Torquay TQ1 2BW; www.admt.org.uk

The Conference of Drama Schools Executive Secretary, PO Box 34252, London NW5 1XJ; www.drama.ac.uk

The National Council for Drama Training 1–7 Woburn Walk, London WC1H 0JJ; www.ncdt.co.uk

Dance UK Battersea Arts Centre, Lavender Hill, London SW11 5TN; www.danceuk.org

Council for Dance Education and Training Old Brewer's Yard, 17–19 Neal Street, London WC2H 9UY; www.cdet.org.uk

Foundation for Community Dance LCB Depot, 31 Rutland Street, Leicester LE1 1RE; www.communitydance.org.uk

Careers

Careers in the Theatre J Richardson. Kogan Page, 1998 (6th edition), £8.99
Creative Careers: Film M Jenkins. Trotman, 2003, £14.99
Creative Careers: Radio T Shillam. Trotman, 2003, £14.99
Creative Careers: Television M Jenkins. Trotman, 2003, £14.99
Getting into Films and Television R Angell. How To Books, 2004, £10.99
Theatre Works N Cohen. Royal National Theatre, 1992, £3.50
Performing Arts Uncovered D Pilgrim. Trotman, 2004, £11.99

The courses   This Guide gives you information to help you narrow down your choice of courses. Your next step is to find out more about the courses that particularly interest you. Prospectuses cover many of the aspects you are most likely to want to know about, but some departments produce their own publications giving more specific details of their courses. University and college websites are shown in TABLE 2a.

You can also write to the contacts listed below.

ALRA Admissions (enquiries@alra.ac.uk), Academy of Live and Recorded Arts, Studio 1, RVP Building, Fitzhugh Grove SW18 3SX

Aberystwyth Nick Strong, Admissions Co-ordinator, University of Wales, Aberystwyth, Parry-Williams Building, Aberystwyth SY23 2AJ

Anglia Ruskin Contact Centre (answers@anglia.ac.uk), Anglia Ruskin University, Bishop Hall Lane, Chelmsford CM1 1SQ

Arts Institute at Bournemouth Admissions (admissions@aib.ac.uk), The Arts Institute at Bournemouth, Wallisdown, Poole, Dorset BH12 5HH

Bangor Admissions Office (admissions@bangor.ac.uk), University of Wales, Bangor LL57 2DG

Bath Spa Admissions Office (enquiries@bathspa.ac.uk), Bath Spa University, Newton Park, Bath BA2 9BN

Drama and Dance

Belfast Admissions Officer, The Queen's University of Belfast, Belfast BT7 1NN

Birmingham Dr R Whyman (j.a.batham@hhs.bham.ac.uk), Admissions Tutor for Drama, University of Birmingham, Edgbaston, Birmingham B15 2TT

Bishop Grosseteste C College Registry (info@bgc.ac.uk), Bishop Grosseteste College, Lincoln LN1 3DY

Brighton Lydia Jones (lj9@brighton.ac.uk), Faculty of Arts and Architecture, University of Brighton, Grand Parade, Brighton BN2 0JY

Bristol Admissions Secretary (kay.russell@bristol.ac.uk), Department of Drama, University of Bristol, Cantocks Close, Woodland Road, Bristol BS8 1UP

Bristol UWE Enquiry and Admissions Service (admissions@uwe.ac.uk), University of the West of England Bristol, Coldharbour Lane, Frenchay, Bristol BS16 1QY

Brunel Admissions and Marketing Officer, Faculty of Arts, Brunel University, Uxbridge UB8 3PH

Buckinghamshire Chilterns UC Admissions Office (admissions@bcuc.ac.uk), Buckinghamshire Chilterns University College, Queen Alexandra Road, High Wycombe HP11 2JZ

Central Lancashire Acting English and theatre studies Dave Pearce (kcorless@uclan.ac.uk), Admissions Tutor, Acting, St Peter's Building; Music theatre Mark Goggins (kcorless@uclan.ac.uk), Admissions Tutor, Music Theatre; Theatre practice Mike McKrell (kcorless@uclan.ac.uk), Admissions Tutor, Theatre Practice, Avenham Building; all at University of Central Lancashire, Preston PR1 2HE

Central S Speech & Drama Academic Registry (enquiries@cssd.ac.uk), Central School of Speech and Drama, Embassy Theatre, Eton Avenue, London NW3 3HY

Chester Dance Amanda Clarkson (performingarts@chester.ac.uk); Drama and theatre studies Ms J Loudon (j.loudon@chester.ac.uk); both at Department of Performing Arts, University of Chester, Parkgate Road, Chester CH1 4BJ

Chichester Dance Cathy Childs (c.childs@chi.ac.uk), Head of Dance; Performing arts Admissions Office (admissions@chi.ac.uk); both at University of Chichester, College Lane, Chichester PO19 6PE

City C Manchester Admissions Office (admissions@ccm.ac.uk), City College Manchester, Sale Road, Northenden, Manchester M23 0DD

Colchester I Course Enquiry Line (info@colchester.ac.uk), Colchester Institute, Sheepen Road, Colchester, Essex CO3 3LL

Coventry Recruitment and Admissions Office (info.rao@coventry.ac.uk), Coventry University, Priory Street, Coventry CV1 5FB

Cumbria I Admissions Officer (admissions@cumbria.ac.uk), Cumbria Institute of the Arts, Brampton Road, Carlisle, Cumbria CA3 9AY

Dartington CA Admissions (enquiries@dartington.ac.uk), Dartington College of Arts, Totnes, Devon TQ9 6EJ

De Montfort Promotion and Recruitment Centre (huadmiss@dmu.ac.uk), Faculty of Humanities, De Montfort University, The Gateway, Leicester LE1 9BH

Derby Student Recruitment Unit (enquiries-admissions@derby.ac.uk), University of Derby, Kedleston Road, Derby DE22 1GB

Doncaster C Information and Guidance Centre (he@don.ac.uk), Doncaster College, Waterdale, Doncaster DN1 3EX

East Anglia Admissions Office (eas.admiss@uea.ac.uk), School of Literature and Creative Writing, University of East Anglia, Norwich NR4 7TJ

East London Student Admissions Office (admiss@uel.ac.uk), University of East London, Docklands Campus, 4–6 University Way, London E16 2RD

Edge Hill Admissions Office (enquiries@edgehill.ac.uk), Edge Hill University, St Helens Road, Ormskirk, Lancashire L39 4QP

Essex Undergraduate Admissions Office (admit@essex.ac.uk), University of Essex, Wivenhoe Park, Colchester CO4 3SQ

Exeter Department Secretary, Department of Drama, School of Drama and Music, University of Exeter, Thornlea, New North Road, Exeter EX4 4JZ

Glamorgan Steve Blandford, School of Humanities and Social Sciences, University of Glamorgan, Pontypridd, Mid Glamorgan CF37 1DL

Glasgow Recruitment, Admissions and Participation Service, Glasgow University, Glasgow G12 8QQ

Goldsmiths Drama and theatre arts Department Secretary (drama@gold.ac.uk), Department of Drama; English and drama Dr Michael Simpson (drama@gold.ac.uk), Department of English and Comparative Literature; both at Goldsmiths University of London, New Cross, London SE14 6NW

Greenwich Enquiry Unit (courseinfo@gre.ac.uk), University of Greenwich, Maritime Greenwich Campus, Old Royal Naval College, London SE10 9LS

Guildhall S Music & Drama Registrar (Admissions) (registry@gsmd.ac.uk), Guildhall School of Music & Drama, Barbican, London EC2Y 8DT

Huddersfield Admissions Tutor (Theatre Studies) (t.moss@hud.ac.uk), University of Huddersfield, Queensgate, Huddersfield HD1 3DH

Hull Drama Mrs Sheila Longbone (s.a.longbone@arts.hull.ac.uk), Faculty of Arts Admissions, University of Hull, Hull HU6 7RX; Theatre and performance studies Scarborough Campus, University of Hull, Filey Road, Scarborough YO11 3AZ

Kent Registry (recruitment@kent.ac.uk), University of Kent, Canterbury, Kent CT2 7NZ

Kingston Student Information and Advice Centre, Cooper House, Kingston University, 40–46 Surbiton Road, Kingston upon Thames KT1 2HX

Laban Admissions Officer (info@laban.org), Laban, Creekside, London SE8 3DZ

Lancaster Nigel Stewart, Theatre Studies Department, Lancaster University, Great Hall Complex, Lancaster LA1 4YW

Leeds Dance Theatre and performance Admissions Co-ordinator (enquiries-pci@leeds.ac.uk), University of Leeds, Bretton Hall, Wakefield WF4 4LG; English literature and theatre studies Dr Francis O'Gorman (undergrad-english@leeds.ac.uk), School of English, University of Leeds, Leeds LS2 9JT

Lincoln Admissions (admissions@lincoln.ac.uk), University of Lincoln, Brayford Pool, Lincoln LN6 7TS

Liverpool Hope Admissions (admission@hope.ac.uk), Liverpool Hope University, Hope Park, Liverpool L16 9JD

LIPA Admissions (admissions@lipa.ac.uk), Liverpool Institute for Performing Arts, Mount Street, Liverpool L1 9HF

Liverpool John Moores Student Recruitment Team (recruitment@ljmu.ac.uk), Liverpool John Moores University, Roscoe Court, 4 Rodney Street, Liverpool L1 2TZ

London Metropolitan Admissions Office (admissions@londonmet.ac.uk), London Metropolitan University, 166–220 Holloway Road, London N7 8DB

London South Bank Admissions Office, London South Bank University, 103 Borough Road, London SE1 0AA

Loughborough Dr Gordon Ramsay (g.p.ramsay@lboro.ac.uk), Loughborough University, Loughborough, Leicestershire LE11 3TU

Manchester Undergraduate Recruitment and Admissions Office, University of Manchester, Oxford Road, Manchester M13 9PL

Manchester Metropolitan Acting Ms N Dowling, Department of Communications Media, Faculty of Art and Design, Manchester Metropolitan University, Mabel Tylecote Building, Cavendish Street, Manchester M15 6BG; Contemporary theatre and performance Jane Turner (j.c.turner@mmu.ac.uk), Course Leader BA Contemporary Theatre and Performance; Dance Drama Graham Shrubsole (g.shrubsole@mmu.ac.uk), Course Leader BA Joint Honours (Arts); both at Manchester Metropolitan University, Alsager, Cheshire ST7 2HL

Marjon Admissions Officer (admissions@marjon.ac.uk), Marjon – The College of St Mark and St John, Derriford Road, Plymouth PL6 8BH

Middlesex Admissions Enquiries (admissions@mdx.ac.uk), Middlesex University, North London Business Park, Oakleigh Road South, London N11 1QS

Mountview ATA Enquiries (enquiries@mountview.ac.uk), Mountview Academy of Theatre Arts, Ralph Richardson Memorial Studios, Clarendon Road, Wood Green N22 6SF

Newman C Admissions Registrar (registry@newman.ac.uk), Newman College, Genners Lane, Bartley Green, Birmingham B32 3NT

North East Wales I Admissions Office (enquiries@newi.ac.uk), North East Wales Institute, NEWI Plas Coch, Mold Road, Wrexham LL11 2AW

Northampton Admissions Office (admissions@northampton.ac.uk), University of Northampton, Park Campus, Broughton Green Road, Northampton NN2 7AL

Northumbria Admissions (ar.admissions@northumbria.ac.uk), School of Art, University of Northumbria, Lipman Building, Newcastle upon Tyne NE1 8ST

Oxford Brookes Admissions Office (admissions@brookes.ac.uk), Oxford Brookes University, Headington, Oxford OX3 0BP

Peterborough RC Information Centre (info@peterborough.ac.uk), Peterborough Regional College, Park Crescent, Peterborough PE1 4DZ

Plymouth Admissions, Faculty of Arts and Education, University of Plymouth, Earl Richards Road North, Exeter EX2 6AS

Portsmouth Humanities Admissions Office, University of Portsmouth, Park Building, King Henry I Street, Portsmouth PO1 2DZ

Queen Margaret Admissions Office (admissions@qmuc.ac.uk), Queen Margaret University, Mucklets Road, Craighall, Musselburgh EH21 6TT

Queen Mary Katherine Hicks (k.hicks@qmul.ac.uk), School of English and Drama, Queen Mary University of London, London E1 4NS

Reading Dr Alastair Phillips (a.w.e.phillips@reading.ac.uk), Department of Film and Drama, University of Reading, Woodlands Avenue, Earley, Reading RG6 1HY

Roehampton Enquiries Office (enquiries@roehampton.ac.uk), Roehampton University, Roehampton Lane, London SW15 5PU

Rose Bruford C Admissions Office (enquiries@bruford.ac.uk), Rose Bruford College, Lamorbey Park, Sidcup, Kent DA15 9DF

Royal Academy of Dance Registrar (faculty@rad.ac.uk), Royal Academy of Dance, 36 Battersea Square, London SW11 3RA

Royal Holloway Dr Chris Megson (chris.megson@rhul.ac.uk), Department of Drama and Theatre, Royal Holloway, University of London, Egham, Surrey TW20 0EX

Royal Scottish A Music & Drama Assistant Registrar (registry@rsamd.ac.uk), Royal Scottish Academy of Music and Drama, 100 Renfrew Street, Glasgow G2 3DB

Royal Welsh C Music & Drama Drama Admissions Officer (drama.admissions@rwcmd.ac.uk), Royal Welsh College of Music and Drama, Cathays Park, Cardiff CF10 3ER

St Martin's C Student Enquiries and Admissions Manager, St Martin's College, Lancaster LA1 3JD

St Mary's C Registry (admit@smuc.ac.uk), St Mary's College, Strawberry Hill, Twickenham TW1 4SX

Salford Roy Humphrey (r.humphrey@salford.ac.uk), School of Media, Music and Performance, University of Salford, Salford M4 4WT

Sheffield Student Recruitment and Admissions (ask@sheffield.ac.uk), University of Sheffield, 9 Northumberland Road, Sheffield S10 2TT

Southampton Solent Student Admissions (admissions@solent.ac.uk), Southampton Solent University, East Park Terrace, Southampton SO14 0RT

Staffordshire Derrick Cameron (d.f.l.cameron@staffs.ac.uk), Admissions Tutor, Faculty of Arts, Media and Design, Staffordshire University, PO Box 661, College Road, Stoke-on-Trent ST4 2XW

Sunderland Student Recruitment (student-helpline@sunderland.ac.uk), University of Sunderland, Chester Road, Sunderland SR1 3SD

Surrey Dr J R Giersdorf (dance@surrey.ac.uk), Admissions Tutor, Dance Studies, University of Surrey, Guildford GU2 7XH

Sussex Admissions Officer (ug.admissions@english.sussex.ac.uk), Drama Studies, University of Sussex, Falmer, Brighton BN1 9SH

Swansea IHE Registry (enquiry@sihe.ac.uk), Swansea Institute of Higher Education, Mount Pleasant, Swansea SA1 6ED

Thames Valley Learning Advice Centre (learning.advice@tvu.ac.uk), Thames Valley University, St Mary's Road, Ealing, London W5 5RF

Trinity C (Carmarthen) Recruitment (registry@trinity-cm.ac.uk), Trinity College Carmarthen, College Road, Carmarthen SA31 3EP

UC Suffolk HE Recruitment and Admissions (info@ucs.ac.uk), University Campus Suffolk, Ipswich IP4 1LT

UCE Birmingham Faculty of Law, Humanities and Social Sciences, Dawson Building, University of Central England in Birmingham, Perry Barr, Birmingham B42 2SU

Ulster Mr J King, School of Media and Performing Arts, University of Ulster, Coleraine BT52 1SA

University of the Arts London Central Registry (c.anderson@arts.ac.uk), University of the Arts London, 65 Davies Street, London W1K 5DA

Wales (UWIC) Marketing and Student Recruitment (admissions@uwic.ac.uk), University of Wales Institute, Cardiff, PO Box 377, Western Avenue, Llandaff CF5 2SG

Warwick Dr Nicholas Whybrow, School of Theatre Studies, University of Warwick, Coventry CV4 7AL

Winchester Course Enquiries and Applications, University of Winchester, West Hill, Winchester SO22 4NR

Wolverhampton Dance practice and performance Dr Anne Hogan (in6791@wlv.ac.uk), Dance Studies Subject Leader, University of Wolverhampton, Walsall Campus, Gorway Road, Walsall WS1 3BD; Drama and performance Dr Dymphna Callery, Drama Subject Leader, University of Wolverhampton, Wulfruna Street, Wolverhampton WV1 1SB

Worcester Admissions (admissions@worc.ac.uk), University of Worcester, Henwick Grove, Worcester WR2 6AJ

York St John Assistant Registrar, Admissions (admissions@yorksj.ac.uk), York St John College, Lord Mayor's Walk, York YO31 7EX

The CRAC Series of Degree Course Guides

Series 1

Architecture, Planning and Surveying

Business, Management and Economics

Classics, Theology and Religious Studies

Engineering

English, Media Studies and American Studies

Hospitality, Tourism, Leisure and Sport

Mathematics, Statistics and Computer Science

Music, Drama and Dance

Physics and Chemistry

Sociology, Anthropology, Social Policy and
Social Work

Series 2

Agricultural Sciences and Food Science and
Technology

Art and Design Studies and History of Art and
Design

Biological Sciences

Environmental Sciences

Geography and Geological Sciences

History, Archaeology and Politics

Law and Accountancy

Medical and Related Professions

Modern Languages and European Studies

Psychology, Philosophy and Linguistics

Trotman Editorial and Publishing Team

Editorial Mina Patria, Editorial Director; Jo Jacomb, Editorial Manager; Ian Turner, Production Editor
Production Ken Ruskin, Head of Manufacturing and Logistics; James Rudge, Production Artworker
Advertising and Sales Tom Lee, Commercial Director; Sarah Talbot, Advertising Manager
Sales and Marketing Sarah Lidster, Marketing Manager
Cover design XAB and James Rudge